*of laughter
and
tears*

# OF LAUGHTER
## *and tears*

a memoir
Sarah K. Joaquin

San Francisco, California

Copyright 2007
by the estate of Sarah K. Joaquin

First Edition

Editor: Gloria Castro Kismadi
Book Design: Edwin Lozada

ISBN 978-0-9712066-5-6
ISBN 0-9712066-5-1
Library of Congress Control Number: 2006939711

*All rights reserved. No part of this publication may be reproduced or distributed in any form or by any means, or stored in a data base or retrieval system, without the prior written permission of the publisher or the estate of Sarah K. Joaquin.*

Carayan Press
PO Box 31816
San Francisco, California
94131-0816
www.carayanpress.com
carayan@carayanpress.com

Printed in the USA

ARKIPELAGO Books
1010 Mission Street
San Francisco, CA 94103 USA
www.arkipelagobooks.com

# ACKNOWLEDGEMENT

As with any worthwhile endeavor, such as the writing of an autobiography, there are individuals who rallied for the support of such a project, putting their best efforts in the hope that their contributions could somehow enhance the content of the book.

It is all the more significant in this particular situation because Sarah passed on quite suddenly while she was still working on her autobiography. Therefore, we, her children, have been tasked with seeing to it that the book is published.

*We would like to thank:*

- Officers of the Likas Pamana and Bahaghari Productions (both co-founded by Sarah), Oscar Bunoan, Hubert Santayana, and Julius Jose; Emmie Batulan, Menchit Lagdameo-Stull and Lem Ramos.

- The editorial and administrative staff of *The Manila Mail* led by chief editor and co-founder Albert Alfaro and Fred de la Rosa, Atty. Wary Azarcon, Jon Melegrito, Bing Branigin and Egai Detera. Sarah's columns that appeared in *The Manila Mail* helped prompt the recollection of important events that found their way into the book.

- Enrique and Rosario Joaquin and family, Jimmy Carino, CEO & owner of Forex Cargo for their unfailing moral support towards the publication of the book.

- Editha Butler, Sarah's close friend, who first edited the manuscript when it was still a "work in progress," yet unfinished when Sarah passed away.

- Chit de Jesus, VP of Forex Cargo; Manny Beldemor, painter; Judge Jim Halpern, Myn Valentin Taylor, Jorge Ortoll, Lino Reyes, Conchita Razon, Joan Orendain and Reme Grefalda, Emmie Batulan, Becky Patsibigan who contributed their pieces to the book.

- Chito Corotan, David Calderon, Greg Lazo, Joe Subido who was constantly close to Sarah as she was struggling to finish the book despite her deteriorating health; Dr. Pio Poblete and nurse Jacqueline Newgen-Smith who helped care for Sarah.

- Gloria Castro Kismadi, who edited Tony's book *Simple Glories* and who despite her very heavy schedule in Jakarta, Indonesia did not hesitate to accede to our request for her to edit Sarah's book. In the process of editing, Gloria saw the need for critical and major changes not only in format but in the need to add additional features from Sarah's life that was not mentioned before, thanks to Dino who supplied most of them. So, all three, Gloria, Fred and Tony had to collaborate and rewrite a greater part of the manuscript.

☞Dino de la Rosa, eldest son of Jojo was the perennial companion of Sarah the whole time she was living in Virginia and with her advancing age, Dino became more valuable to his grandmother, accompanying her wherever she went – especially during those rehearsal days for the plays. Dino's familiarity with the finer details in Sarah's activities proved to be priceless when they were included in the book.

*The following donated funds for the publication of the book:*

Clarita Agorilla
Pilar Arpon
Lily and Loleng Bacaoco
Manuel Baldemor
Evelyn and Oscar Bunoan
Lita Carlos
Balbino and Sally Hernando
Gregorio and Gigi Macabenta
Sonia Micklat
Pete and Boots Anson Roa
Ambassador and Mrs. Eduardo Romualdez
Tony and Cristina Romualdez
Teresa Joaquin-Serrao
Herminia Ubaldo-Smith
Perfecto and Cecile Yasay

☞To our relatives and friends who took pains in sourcing old photographs that were necessary for inclusion in the book, as well as to others whose names may have been overlooked, our heartfelt gratitude.

*Antonio, Lourdes, Josefina and Jose Joaquin*

# INTRODUCTION

## *My Sister Sarah*

She came into my life late in the 1920s, marrying my brother Ping, when he was Manila's vaudeville King of Jazz, and I was an aspiring writer, age 12. I had a portfolio of sketches: the story of a child beginning to observe and ask questions. She took charge of those early effusions—corrected the English, edited the style, and sent off the more promising ones to her friends in the magazine world. She knew everybody! In this way, I was first published: a slight vignette of mine titled—if my memory serves me right—"Shooting Stars."

She was also the first to write about me: a droll article titled "My Brother Nick" that appeared during the war and aroused the wrath of the then high priest of Philippine letters: Federico Mangahas, who rightly protested that a serious journal—Philippine Review—edited by Vicente Albano Pacis, should waste space on somebody who had only a handful of tales and verses to his name. "Who?" asked Mr. Managahas, is Nick Joaquin?" But that only gave Sarah a stick with which to whoop Mr. Mangahas, a good friend of hers.

After the war, she was with a theater group that put on plays like García Lorca's *House of Bernarda Alba* and was criticized for not putting on native drama. So Sarah asked me to write them a play, a three-act play. I demurred. I was no longer a playwright and wouldn't know how to dramatize action or build up dialogue. "Just do what you can," said Sarah, "and I'll edit it."

So I wrote *A Portrait of the Artist as a Filipino*, with her in mind doing the role of Paula.

Sarah went through the huge bundle of manuscript and shook her head. "But this is impossible!" she cried. I agreed with her and dumped my play on a shelf where it gathered dust until it was discovered by Daisy Hontiveros-Avellana. The rest, as they say, is history.

Years later, I wrote another play for Sarah: *The Beatas* where she was to have played the role of Mother Francisca. Sarah was eager to do it... but again, it was not to be. She had to migrate to America. Sarah would have been terrific as Mother Francisca, that great dynamic feminist of 17$^{th}$ Century Manila.

When I think of Sarah, I see dynamos. Physically, intellectually, spiritually—she's a dynamo. And I speak from a knowledge of her dating back to my childhood. I'm happy to hear she is still effervescing. I doubt she'll ever burn out.

*Nick Joaquin*
November 1999

*for
my family
and friends*
xo

## Chapter One

"Sarah!" The voice reached me as I was just about to pull myself to a higher branch. I was halfway up the tree, but I recognized the tone and I scampered down as quickly as I could, scratching my knee in the process.

The voice belonged to my father, Balbino Yuson Kabigting. *Tatay*, I called him then. He was a strict disciplinarian, and while his manner was gentle, at times he could also be stern. If I grew up with the freedom to express myself in words and in action, it was all because of him. No one else had a greater influence on me in my younger years, and even when I was older. He took me everywhere, and I got to know all his friends and the people he worked with. He goaded me to engage in debates with him and laughed heartily at my various attempts at imitation and mimicry. I adored him! I wanted to be, if anything, like him.

But I was also sensitive to the different vocal tones he used that showed his moods, and this time, I thought I had to get to him as fast as I could. Tatay never raised his voice at me except in anger and from the way he called my name, I knew that this time, there was no way I could charm him out of this mood.

"I wonder what I've done now," I asked myself as I hurried up the stairs, taking them two at a time. From the way Tatay sounded, I was in for a scolding. Running in to meet him, I realized that I had forgotten to put on my slippers. I had removed them to climb the tree, but it was too late to go back for them now. I knew that he would also have something to say about that.

The moment I saw what he had in his hands, my heart sank. *Tatay* was really upset. He was holding the slingshot I had been looking for earlier. "Where did you get this? Where did you learn to use it?"

His voice came out slowly, but there was no warmth in the way he spoke. I always cringed every time he sounded like this for I immediately knew he was displeased with something I had said or done.

"Answer me!" It was a command.

"Kiko, gave me the *tirador*," I said, my voice trembled not from fear but more from knowing that I had upset him.

"From now on you are not to play with slingshots! Not at any time! When you have one in your hands you are tempted to practice on moving animals, especially small ones, like birds and lizards! Your mother is horrified! Why do you think I put that drinking fountain out in the garden? So you could shoot at the birds that she loves?"

Then and there *Tatay* lectured me on the bad habit of shooting birds with a slingshot or *tirador*. He said we should love birds as we loved our dogs. Birds, he said, never did anything wrong. They were made to do only one thing, and that was to sing for God and for men, and they did that with all their heart. "We should be more like them, and not go around bringing them harm!" he said.

When the lecture was over, *Tatay* happened to look down at my feet. I was tired and had started to fidget and that's when he noticed I did not have my sandals on. "And why are you in your bare feet?" he asked, his voice rising once more. "How many times have I told you that you are never to go anywhere without shoes or slippers on! You can get sick, or hurt yourself! When will you learn?"

"I forgot to put them on when I hurried down from the tree. I tried to get here as fast as I could." I tried to defend myself. I expected another lecture on going around in my bare feet, but instead, he turned abruptly and stomped off.

After that lecture, my friends and I just tried to catch birds and put them in cages so we could watch them and hear them sing, but when *Tatay* found out we were doing that, he said it was wrong too, because birds were not meant to live in cages. They were made to fly freely.

Besides, if we caught one and put it in a cage, it might have some nestlings waiting for her to come home so they could have supper.

I once boasted to him that I could climb a guava tree faster than a monkey and could kill a house lizard with amazing accuracy with my *tirador*. *Tatay* was not impressed. Instead, he said, "And do you think that makes you better than them?" No small creature would have a chance against anyone whose mind was made up to kill it, and climbing trees faster than a monkey was not a feat to be proud of, he said, it only meant I was not any different from them. It was quite easy to run up and down the fruit trees, because the tree trunks grew in a reclining position, he said. In most farms, fruit trees were usually formed this way as they were growing so that it would be easier to pick the fruit when they were ready to be harvested and brought to market. So what was there to be proud of?

Shortly after this episode, before Christmas, 1915, my father brought me with him to Manila to see his friend, *Doña* Librada Avelino, who was then the director of *Centro Escolar de Señoritas*. At that time, I did not know that I was brought there so that *Doña* Librada could look me over and get to know me to see if I was ready for enrolment in the new school year. But even as I stood there while they were talking about me, somehow I sensed that the days of my carefree childhood were coming to an end.

*Tatay* was Balbino Yuson Kabigting and *Nanay* was Carlota Carlos. I was their fourth child, but the three born before me unfortunately died, victims of the high infant mortality prevalent in those days. Superstition, however, attributed their deaths to their having been given fancy names instead of saint's names. So, when I was born as the church bells of San Isidro, Nueva Ecija, were ringing to announce the Mass in celebration of the Feast of the Epiphany, the day commemorating the visit of the three kings: Gaspar, Melchor, and Balthasar, to the child Jesus in Bethlehem, my mother was adamant that I had to be given the name of the saint honored for that day, according to the Catholic calendar. Since there were three saints, *Nanay* asked *Tatay* to make the choice. He chose Balthasara so we would have the same initials, B.K., for which I am grateful. Can you imagine my having to go through life with the name Gaspara or Melchora? It was also *Tatay* who shortened the name to Sarah after hearing people calling me "Sarang", the "ng" being commonly attached to the names of children then. *Papá* said "Sarah" also sounded more dignified and gave my name a Spanish sound.

When I was growing up, I was often told that I had brought good luck to my parents because after I was born, my father passed the First Grade Civil Service examination that he needed to qualify for the job of provincial treasurer. His assignment to Malolos was the first step in his chosen career. Thus, my first memories were of Malolos when I was about five years old.

As far back as I can remember, my playmates were all boys, although my mother tried as best she could to make me look like a prim and proper little girl. She would part my straight, shoulder-length hair from front to back and braid each side, then roll them up and clip them over each ear so that I would always look neat and tidy. It is a wonder that with all my escapades, *Nanay* never made a complaint over my torn clothes but would continue to mend all the rips and tears from climbing all those trees and sliding down hillsides. When we went to parties or to church on Sundays, she would put a bow, the same color as my dress, on top of each coiled braid. I remember seeing photographs of myself, my chubby face with the ribbons on my braids, larger than the coils, almost hiding my small nose. I could only think of myself as looking like a rabbit. Luckily, it was not long before I managed to escape all that care once my younger sister, Nene, was born.

*Tatay* often remarked that I was very gregarious. Whenever we went to my maternal grandfather's house in San Miguel, Bulacan, for the traditional family Christmas gathering, I would first greet everyone and chat with them before running off to play with the neighbor's boys and my two cousins, Ireneo and Meneleo, sons of my mother's only brother, Ignacio.

After Christmas, we would usually go to the neighboring barrio of Sibul, where my great uncle Agripino, a little older than my grandfather, lived in a house much too big for himself and his godson who was his only companion. For us children, it was a big holiday for it meant a fairly long ride in one of the horse-drawn vehicles of that time when motor cars were only for the moneyed class.

In those days, transportation was always animal-drawn, either by horse or carabao. For big loads, there was the *carretón,* a square, low platform with foot high sides made of bamboo slats tied close together. This was drawn by a huge, strong and uncomplaining carabao, no matter how heavy the burden, but it was an awfully slow way to get anywhere. The safety of the *carretón* was undisputable except for those times when it would tilt because the terrain would be higher on one side. If the carabao took it a bit faster than usual, the *carretón* could topple over and bury its passengers under. So those of us who rode in it had to be sure to shift from side to side to keep the vehicle in balance. It was fun to ride in the *carretón* when we were not in a hurry, for a lot of patience was necessary to accept its speed. As children, we didn't really care. It was more fun to sit on the floor of the *carretón* and tell stories, sing songs or make jokes. We were children and we didn't know the meaning of time or having to rush off somewhere. Our days seemed to go from one to the other without worry or care.

A faster vehicle that could carry a lighter load was the *carretela,* a flat, wooden, horse-drawn rig that seated four to six people in comfort. It was always a trick to get to the back seat because our weight would lower the back and tip up the front end of the *carretela* and if we were not holding on tight, we could find ourselves sprawled over the back seat.

A little higher in the social scale and more popular was the *calesa*, sometimes called a *caromata*, a smaller vehicle, drawn by a single horse where three, average-size persons could sit comfortably. The luxury vehicles were the *carruajes* with the *Victoria* being considered as top of the line. The *Victoria* was usually pulled by at least two Arabian stallions. It had two rows of seats facing each other, the one at the back of the horses right under the high *pescante* where two uniformed drivers sat during the trip. The driver seated on a tall stool on the right side controlled the horse, or horses, running on the right side; the other driver in a smaller, lower chair was in charge of the left ones. This was the origin of the order *de mano* directed to the driver on the right for a right turn and *de silla* for the one on the left for a left turn. Even after so many years after the Spanish were gone, the idiom remained in the dialect.

To get to the *barrio* of Sibul, which was a popular summer resort for wealthy families in Manila because of its medicinal waters, the family rode in two *carretelas*. Most of the time, I rode with my cousins, Irining and Meneleo with all the packages of food and suitcases of clothes. My mother and *Tío* Ignacio, her younger brother, were with my younger sister, Nene, and my cousin, Poying, *Tío* Ignacio's daughter. With a beautiful name like Florencia, I don't understand, to this day, how she ended up with such an unglamorous nickname.

I have very fond memories of *Lolo* Agring's large piece of land—two hectares, we were told. We never could see where it ended; it seemed so vast. In the front part, facing the street, stood this big house with four bedrooms. The first floor was a big store where almost everything that any human being needed could be bought. My granduncle's name was Agripino Carlos and we called him *Lolo* Agring for short. I have to put in a word for him because he was quite a character. *Lolo* Agring was very proud of his being a member of the Katipunan, in the first Philippine army that fought against the Spanish rulers. *Lolo* Agring's uniform and rifle hung in one corner of the big living room to attest to that.

The Katipunan was an organization formed by Andrés Bonifacio shortly after José Rizal was arrested and exiled. Its sole purpose was to win independence from Spain, but at the start, it functioned more as a secret society. While the nationalist movement began with a closed circle of *ilustrados* such as the likes of Rizal and Mabini, it got to have a more popular base of support. With the idea of an independent *Filipinas* catching fire, men and women from the peasantry and the lower to middle class income groups joined the army and by the time it began its revolt against Spain in 1895, it had some 30,000 members. The rebels were poorly led, however, and had more courage than equipment and military know-how to help them achieve their goal, not to mention the break that took place between the leadership—Aguinaldo and Bonifacio.

To *Lolo* Agring, his participation in the fight for an independent Philippines was something in which he took great pride. He had endless stories to tell us children, and often he repeated them to us. He wasn't about to let anyone forget the courage of the first Filipino soldiers.

Everyone in the small community of Sibul knew *Lolo* Agring. He was well-liked because in his store was everything that anyone could possibly need in the house—food, drinks, herbal medicine, as well as simple first-aid medical requirements. He also had garden and farm tools, and, of course, plant fertilizer. As the saying goes, name it, he had it.

As busy as the front of the house was, *Lolo* Agring's backyard was a solace of peace and quiet. To me it was a beautiful, picture-story garden. There were *sampaguitas, jazmín, ilang-ilang* and *dama de noche*, all of which brought to the house their individual sweet scents. *Lolo* Agring, knew precisely where to plant them so that one fragrance would not overpower another. The *jazmín* and the *sampaguita* filled the air with their sweet and soft perfume in the back patio; the *dama de noche* below the bedroom windows gave people scented night dreams and the *ilang-ilang* tree out in the fieldas near the beehives and banana trees, was a delight to those who wanted to go a bit farther to catch the cool, refreshing breeze.

Scattered around *Lolo* Agring's small rice paddies were several fruit trees which my cousins, Meneling and Irining taught me to climb. Many an afternoon, when the blazing sun kept the adults inside to enjoy their siestas, we would be up the guava tree eating the ripe fruit or getting some of its leaves for *Lolo* Agring to boil and use as disinfectant for minor cuts or skin diseases that were brought to him for treatment. There was a big mango tree, a few tamarind and *camachile* trees and soon I was scurrying up those trees even faster than Meneling and Irining. Once, *Nanay* saw me scurrying as fast as I could up those trees and she complained to *Tatay*. She did not like it at all. Other than the possible danger that every mother sees, she also told *Tatay* that I was growing up to be a tomboy. *Lolo* Agring, on the other hand, saw how much fun I was having and called me *ang aking magandang unggoy*.\*

In my mother's eyes, I was getting too wild and undisciplined. All my playmates in the neighborhood were boys and I don't think they ever thought that I was not one of them. It was *Tatay*, though, who wanted me to grow up to be a genteel, refined young lady with a good command of Spanish—at that time the language of the elite. *Nanay*, while worrying about my unladylike behavior, thought, however, that it was too early to worry about turning me into a lady. I suspect she did not really want to think about my leaving home so soon to become properly educated.

But my father had already made up his mind. I was enrolled at the *Centro Escolar de Señoritas* and I would be leaving for Manila in the

---

\**My pretty monkey.*

following school year which began in June. The *Directora*, his very good friend *Doña* Librada Avelino was someone *Tatay* knew and could trust to bring me up properly even though I was only seven years old. I would be an *interna*. For months, the preparations for my leaving occupied the whole household. I was somewhat oblivious to all this and continued to enjoy my freedom but every time I would be called in for a fitting, or I would see how everyone was bustling around to get things ready for me, and my heart would sink. I had no idea what it was like to leave home, and what was to become of me.

I would think of having to leave my playmates with whom I had spent such carefree days, and I would feel bad. From them I had learned to shoot marbles, climb trees, find birds' nests and shoot with a slingshot. Most painful of all, I would be missing *Tatay* who was my peaceful anchor, especially at the end of the day when he would tell me stories before I went to bed. By that time, *Nanay* was too busy taking care of my baby sister, Nene, and while she may have had too little time for me before that, she would call me now and then and give me a hug and brush my hair back with her hands. "Always be a good girl," she would whisper, holding my face in her hands. I think she, too, was starting to have a few regrets about letting go of me so soon.

## Chapter Two

*Centro Escolar de Señoritas* was founded in 1908 by four young, enterprising, forward-looking Filipino ladies, and an equally progressive and risk-taking young lawyer. At a time when education was a prime consideration and the economy was good enough so that concerned parents looked for schools that were known for quality, *Centro Escolar de Señoritas* opened its doors to accommodate the daughters of a rising upper middle class.

The school rapidly gained prestige, not only in the Philippine archipelago but also in neighboring Asian countries, as the best place for young girls to get a well-rounded education in arts and letters. It quickly succeeded in getting a reputation for quality education and the training of young girls in good social manners and right conduct according to internationally accepted standards of behavior among the elite of those times.

At its head was *Doña* Librada Avelino, a courageous and intelligent lady who believed that women were created with the same quality of brains as men—a terrifyingly advanced concept in the predominantly male macho society of the Philippines. In due time, women would take their rightful places beside men, but *Doña* Librada did not believe that it should happen later rather than sooner. She stressed that the basic elements for women were to have a solid academic background and at the same time become the guardians and advocates of values and models of correct moral and social behavior. Sharing her dreams and ambitions were Carmen de Luna, Felisa Francisco, Maria Francisco de Villaceran—one of the first women lawyers in this country—and Josue Soncuya. This ambitious institution had considerably high tuition fees for those times, but they were not beyond the reach of upper middle class Filipino families so that so that the up-and-coming elite sent their daughters to the *Centro*.

It was to the *Centro* that *Tatay* entrusted me with complete confidence that I would turn out to be what he ideally wanted me to be. This was one more proof that he knew exactly what he wanted for me, and he was right. Having spent ten of my most formative years there, I attribute much of the shaping of my character and personality to *Doña* Librada and my other mentors who guided me in the proper direction with strict and consistent discipline softened with gentle patience.

That June day, with all my belongings packed in trunks and suitcases finally came and there was no turning back. I had been dreading it, finally accepting the fact that I was going away. I only needed to take a look at all that luggage and know that I would be away for a long time. Before that, I had already told my friends I would not be starting school with them. I saw them outside waiting to wave me off but I did not want to look at them nor say goodbye. I did not want them to see my tears. Saying goodbye to *Nanay* and my little sister was painful enough. While I had not really spent too much time at home with them throughout the summer, I was starting to regret that and I wondered when I would see them again. I could feel my heart beating very fast as I kissed Nene first, and then *Nanay*. She hugged me tightly and I saw the tears flowing down her cheeks, but she never said a word. Perhaps this is one reason why I find leave-takings somewhat traumatic.

Then *Tatay* and I were on our way. During the trip I was very quiet. *Tatay*, teased me about not being as talkative and curious as I normally would have been but he must have sensed how I felt for he said, "You don't have to be sad. I will visit you every other weekend...provided you write me in Spanish, one letter a week." *Tatay* had already been assigned to Bataan before that. It was his first assignment as a full-fledged provincial treasurer. Bataan, in those days, was not within easy reach of Manila, so I knew that he would be making a big sacrifice to come and see me.

To me, leaving home seemed inevitable. *Tatay* and *Nanay* had both prepared me for it. I knew it was coming but why did I not want it? Once, I asked *Tatay* why I had to go to school so far away. "Why can't I just go to school here where all my friends are going?"

"There is so much more for you to learn than what you can find here," he said. "I want to give you the best education so that you can do many things when you are older. The better your education, the more you will be able to do for society. Someday, you will understand."

So, during the trip, while in my heart I was sad, I did not want the tears to show because I felt it would have made *Tatay* feel terrible and disappointed in me. He was sending me away and I had such faith in him that I believed he meant it to be good for me. But I still had no idea what would happen. I think it must have been the very first time that I thought of my future, but I still did not understand it. All I knew was that I was going off to school, far away from my parents whom I would not be seeing for some time. I knew that my life would be different from then on. I felt that I was at the very edge of a world that was familiar and about to enter into something completely new. On the one hand, I was sad, anxious, and a bit afraid, but at the same time, there was a feeling of curiosity over what would happen next.

During the trip, *Tatay* told me that while I would be an *interna,* and I would live in the school, his brother, Salvador—*Tío* Badong—and my mother's brother, Ignacio—*Tío* Ignacio—would be my *encargados* or guardians. They would act on my parents' behalf in case of an emergency. Either one of them could also take me out of school on a Friday afternoon, if I got too lonely and wanted to enjoy some family life. Then on Sundays, I would be brought back. My father's words did not make any sense to me at that time. I could not absorb what he meant as the full understanding of my being left behind became real only when I saw him walking out the door leaving me inside after saying goodbye. I could hardly hold back my tears when I realized that I would not be seeing *Tatay,* whom I loved very much and from whom I had never been separated, for a long time.

*Tatay* also told me he knew several young ladies among the grown-up students in the school who were to graduate three years later, Purificacion Gallego (later Tanchoco) and Beatriz Bautista (later Valero). They had already promised him they would look after me and help me adjust to life at the Centro. But even that made no sense to me then.

The boarders were divided into three groups: *pequeñas,* who were the small ones; the *medianas* who were the teenagers; and the *mayores,* who were already considered adults. Each group had its own dormitory. The one for the *pequeñas,* where I belonged, held sixty beds arranged in three rows of twenty beds each.

The Centro also had students who were given free tuition and board and lodging in exchange for services they rendered to the school, like helping in the kitchen or helping the little ones get dressed or bathed. They were called *agraciadas.* In our dorm there was one *agraciada* for every five children. They helped us put on our uniforms, they did our hair or simply watched us dress ourselves, lending a hand only when we asked for their help.

At that time we had four types of uniforms that had to be available any time any of them was needed. First, there was the linen-like white dress with a wide collar and belt and two front pockets, all with pink piping. This was the uniform worn to class, which, I believe, is still in use until now. Then there was the one in pink satin, with a square neckline with a collar trimmed with lace and with six mother-of-pearl buttons in front. This was our Sunday uniform which we wore for Mass at the San Sebastian Church. The gala uniform was pink thick *crêpe de chine* with long sleeves trimmed beautifully with Brussels lace.

For the adult students the gala uniform was a Filipino *terno*, the festive costume of the women in our country, consisting of an ankle-length skirt with a short train which was pinned at the side, and a blouse of pineapple fiber starched stiff with butterfly sleeves that had the school logo with the words *Ciencia y Virtud* embroidered neatly in silver letters. Looking back, I remember a feeling of hope then that someday I would qualify to wear that gala *terno*.

In the first few weeks of my stay at the Centro, I felt miserable. The routine was so different from my home life that I felt I was being punished for something I did not do. I could not understand why *Tatay* allowed this to happen to me. If he really loved me, why was he so insistent that I go to school in a place like this. Or maybe, he didn't realize what I was going through. I made up my mind to tell him when I saw him.

Every morning at five, except on Saturdays, we were awakened by the nasty ringing of a bell which the *inspectora*, the one in charge of the dorm, clanged loudly around the big room. As soon as we heard this bell we had to immediately fall on our knees beside our beds facing the big crucifix on the altar at one end of the room. Then we did the morning prayers, which lasted for fifteen minutes. After prayers, we were herded to the bathrooms. Some showered or did their bathroom needs while the rest prepared books and bags to be ready to pick up after breakfast at seven o'clock. For the *pequeñas,* the *agraciadas* were around to help those who still could not comb their hair or get dressed on their own. I was one of those who needed help. My hair was down to my shoulders so Felisa, the sweet, good-natured one assigned to me, sometimes fixed my hair in two braids, pinned them over my ears and stuck a pink bow on each side.

After about six weeks I had adjusted to the rigorous life like a soldier who had fallen in step with his comrades. It was difficult at the start for a seven-year-old, but I suppose, like most children who are usually resilient when it comeas to change, I got used to the routine and no longer looked at life at the Centro as a punishment. I had made many friends and was happy to be there.

My father kept his promise and visited me every other week provided I wrote him a letter in Spanish once a week. So I never failed to write him every Saturday after the "laundry hour" when we gave our dirty clothes to the *lavandera,* the laundry women, and got back our clean ones. Every time he came, *Tatay* would bring the letters I sent him with all the corrections. It was also at that time that I started to call him *Papá*. Little did I know that he kept the very first letter I ever sent to him with the salutation I had written: *Mi kerido Papá*. I found out only after he gave it to my husband when I had my first baby.

The days that *Papá* came were truly "feast" days for me. I found out soon enough that these were just as happy events for him. He would take me out and we would go places, or visit with relatives and friends. Inevitably he would ask my mentors how I was doing in class and whether I behaved as expected, and the answer was invariably "very bright but very naughty." And that was the reputation I was stuck with all throughout grade school.

It was very clear that the school wanted to make genteel ladies out of us. We were taught Bible History and catechism and were brought up to be good Roman Catholics. The San Sebastian Church located on R. Hidalgo Street, that venerable basilica made of steel in the Gothic style and whose spires majestically point up to the heavens, was the temple of our Faith. It was there that at age nine, together with fifteen other girls my age, I received the Holy Eucharist for the very first time. All of us wore immaculately white long-sleeved dresses with matching veils and gloves and crowned with *sampaguita* blossoms, their sweet fragrance filling the church rows where we sat. That was one of the happiest moments of my childhood.

The school also saw to it that we were taught as many languages as we could learn. I thought it was a crazy idea at that time and I said so to my father who told me that some day, later in my life, that knowledge would come in handy. He was so right...as always.

During the week we were allowed to speak English or Spanish anywhere, even in the classrooms. No Filipino dialect, however, was to be spoken anywhere. Any violation incurred meant punishment in the form of delayed deliveries of letters from home, or having to spend the recreation hour alone in the dorm. On those occasions when we did not know how to say something in correct English or Spanish we would first look furtively around and then speak in a whisper. We all thought it was quite silly, but it got us to speak English most of the time. Weekends were a bit more difficult because we not only allowed to speak in any dialect, we couldn't even use English. Weekends meant using Spanish, just pure Spanish. This meant that the less courageous and more timid remained silent as long as they could or when they really had to say something they said it in what we called "carabao Spanish." I had a little edge over many of my friends because my father always spoke to me in Spanish. My mother was much more of a nationalist because she often talked to me and to the maids in Tagalog which was the dialect she grew up with and used most of her life.

I got very high grades in my academic subjects especially in English grammar and literature. What may have helped me was that I was such a voracious reader. I loved books, and by the time I was in the fourth grade I had already read *Treasure Island, The Prince and the Pauper, The Adventures of Huckleberry Finn, Little Women,* and many other books that were required reading for high school students. But as good as my grades were in those subjects, my grades in Conduct and Social Forms certainly do not merit mention.

Every Saturday afternoon we had a two-hour "Workshop on Social Forms." We were taught good manners and right conduct, especially table manners, behavior in church, or when speaking with older persons. We learned how to walk and sit like ladies, and how to hold a teacup with our pinkies curled up higher than the other fingers. I remember that I was always afraid I would drop the cup and break it. We were repeatedly told that a refined young lady did not empty a glass full of water in one big gulp no matter how thirsty she might be. This was always very difficult when we came to the table for supper, thirsty after playing vigorous, physical games. Social Forms frowned on ladies who crossed their legs and despised those who smoked. Smoking, we were told, made us look "cheap". We practiced going up the stairs one little step at a time, gracefully, and without haste. I can no longer remember how many times I was punished for running and climbing the stairs, taking them two steps at a time.

When I was in the fourth grade, *Doña* Librada, the *Directora*, had a bright idea. The school had become so popular by then that it was overflowing with boarders from all over the country who were crammed in the three existing dorms. *Doña* Librada started what she called "*internas especiales*" or special boarders who were housed in a luxurious mansion formerly owned by the very wealthy Don Antonio Roxas, a huge, ornate house, situated at the corner of Tanduay and General Solano streets. The board and lodging fee was double that of the regular boarders who lived in the main building on Azcarraga Street.

By that time, my father was a full-fledged provincial treasurer with a considerable increase in salary and my mother helped with the income by selling fruits, sugar and coconuts from the family farm that she managed. My father, learning of *internas especiales* program, decided that I should have a taste of luxurious living. So he enrolled me in the group.

Three of us shared a fairly large-sized room—an Indian girl Shakunthala Zharda, whose parents owned a big store in Cebu City, Rosita Cunanan, a sweet little girl from Pampanga, besides myself. Ours was a corner room that had two windows, one that looked out on Tanduay Street and one that had a good view of the *azotea* or back patio, a common part of large houses in those times and that was so typically Spanish in structure and design. The *azotea* had patterned tile flooring and was surrounded by a carved marble balustrade, which supported a profusion of decorative and flowering plants. I can still remember how the tall sweet scented *jazmín* vine filled the room with its aroma all day long, reminding me of *Lolo* Agring's garden in Sibul Springs. We each had a four-poster bed with soft pink draperies and a white mosquito net that protected us from insect bites during the night. Much later the windows were screened and the nets disappeared.

The routine was the same as it was in the main building, prayers at five-thirty in the morning, then bathroom needs, followed by breakfast. We rode to school—all twenty-four of us—in a big new bus driven by a uniformed driver. We had lunch in a small room near the faculty lounge, away from the main refectory with its sounds of plates and spoons and voices of friends and laughter and fun. After classes, at four o'clock, we were driven home to our "mansion," all of us a little sad because we missed the fun and games we had always enjoyed with our friends, swapping bits of gossip, and stories that took place in the regular dorm. In our "home" we had our own little recreation time before dinner but it was different. There were only six of us of about the same age so we gathered in the huge landscaped garden to talk about the stars that were slowly creeping into the heavens and to breathe the cool evening breeze, but it wasn't the same. After all, how long could we do that before getting completely bored?

Dinner was another elegant affair. The table was absolutely unbelievable. Everything on it was glittering silver, or so we thought until we found out later they were only silver-plated. The plates, the flatware, our serving dishes—all shone brightly above the white linen tablecloth. Our glasses were not glass at all, but little silver goblets that were gold-plated inside, almost like chalices. We made fun of this at the beginning of the school term. Rosita, my roommate, gave a silly answer when the *inspectora*, in charge, asked her why she did not eat her chicken at all. "I am afraid it is made of silver too," she answered in an innocent way, evoking a hearty laugh from all of us and a smirk from *Maestra* Felisa. But, alas, despite all this luxurious comfort and opulence, which we enjoyed, there were many problems.

The school had a regular literary musical program every other month celebrating various occasions and several of the participants came from our group. So we had to be driven back to the main building for rehearsals or we had to stay in and eat with the faculty and be driven home afterwards. I was always among the participants and it was taking a big toll on my health. To remedy this I was given the privilege to stay away from the first two periods in class the next day since I was at the top of the class anyway. Then I was driven to school for the third period.

Another problem, which was more painful, was that our group was fast losing friends. The others looked upon us with a little envy mixed with some loathing. We were sarcastically referred to as the "sacred cows" and were often avoided by those friends whom we liked to be with very much. Divisive lines were forming and it seemed that it was we who suffered most.

"Pooh" they would say, "there go the snootiest snobs in the school." It hurt to be called that by those who at one time were close friends. I even heard it said that the only reason I was getting the highest grades in my class was because I belonged to this group. This I could not accept since I felt I deserved every grade I got. The truth was that there were many students in the main building who were far wealthier but who did not take the advantage offered of living in the "mansion."

We told our parents this but they would not listen. I suppose they had their own reasons.

As Providence would have it, the grandeur did not last long. After three short years the *Directora*, realizing her miscalculation, announced that the program was off. So, like Cinderellas whose golden carriage had turned back into a pumpkin we found ourselves in the old dorms for the new school year.

My mother was very glad. Aside from the fact that she would pay less for my board and lodging, she also did not approve of our being treated differently and thought that we were being brought up as little *chiliads* or high-faluting snobs. So, with that, she put my silver things in storage and made living room pillows out of the expensive drapery. I was jubilant because now all of us could go back to our usual schedules and to our friends.

## *Chapter Three*

As much as I was absorbed in my activities at the *Centro,* by the time Christmas came around, and especially in March when final examinations were facing us, I would already be looking forward to vacation and being with the family once again. I realized then how much I had missed *Papá, Mamá,* and Nene. I would promise myself that I would spend more time with my sister, I almost didn't know her at all since she was still very small when I left the first time to go to school in Manila.

When I was still in the primary grades, school breaks were mostly spent in Manila. The reason was that during those years *Papá* was assigned to different provinces in the southern regions and he did not want me to have to adjust to different places and people during my vacation. We would stay with family in Manila until it was time to go back to school once again. On occasion, however, I would spend my vacations in those different places where he was assigned.

Surigao, on the Island of Mindanao, was the first southern province *Papá* was assigned to. In those years, it was still just one province and had not yet been split into Surigao del Norte and Surigao del Sur. On the first year of his assignment there he came to Manila with my mother and sister. As usual we stayed in the house of *Tío* Ignacio, my mother's brother. Their three-story apartment had space for guests and was also easily accessible to the *tranvía,* the electric streetcar that was the chief means of transportation in the city in those days. After Christmas, New Year and my birthday on the 6th of January, I would be brought back to school while the rest of the family returned to Surigao.

During the long summer break, though, *Papá* would take me to Surigao just to show me the beautiful town by the sea. I was not happy there at first because everyone spoke Cebuano, which I did not understand. In no time at all, however, I learned a big chunk from the neighborhood children with whom I played and I began to enjoy every day that I was there. Unfortunately, I stayed for less than a month as my father was called for an important conference in Manila and he wanted to save on time and expense. Otherwise, he would have to take another trip in June to bring me back to school. I did not really mind the short stay with my mother because she was quite busy anyway with the household chores and the care of my sister and could not attend to me much. My sister was still too young to go outside and play with me. So for the whole month of May I stayed with *Tío* Ignacio's family and we went as usual to my great uncle Agring's farm in Sibul Springs.

In those days, the only means of travel were small boats owned by the Maritima Shipping Lines. The trip took two days and two nights. I was a good sailor and I enjoyed those trips. But there was that one year when a big storm came up and no boat dared to brave the inclement weather. This was in June when I had to be back in school because vacation was over. There was no way I could make it back on time. My teachers were unhappy about what I missed in school and the *Directora* told my father she hoped it would not happen again.

After three and a half years in Surigao my father was sent to Bohol in the Visayas. It was a little bit nearer to Manila but transportation was still only by boat, though shortened to only one and a half days. Once, when I had my summer break there, I had to stay much longer because I got sick at the beginning of June as classes were about to start. *Papá* did not want me away from the family until I had fully recovered from my illness. He petitioned the Bureau of Education to allow me to study in the Tagbilaran Middle School for the first semester after which I would return to the Centro. By the time I left in October, I was already speaking Boholano like a native. Gone were my genteel ways during that time, as I played with the children in school and in the neighborhood every day and learned their language and games.

One vacation that stands out and is clearly etched in my memories were the vacation days that I spent in Santa Cruz, capital of the province of Laguna. I must have been ten or eleven years old when, having no boys in our neighborhood as playmates, I took a liking for a new friend, a girl by the name of Juanita Falcon. Her family was one of the wealthiest in the town. Often, we would get invited to dinner at their house in appreciation for assistance that my father extended to them

There were only two children in the Falcon family—Basilio, the older one and his sister, Juanita. Both of them were also studying in Manila—Basiling in San Juan de Letran College, and Juaning in Saint Scholastica College. Before long, Juaning and I had become very close, and my mother was happiest about this arrangement because having a girl friend meant I would not grow up rough and tumble like I did before when my playmates were all boys. So I was allowed to play with Juaning the whole day and *Mamá* cooked lots of delicious food to send them as compensation for my having lunch with them all the time.

Juaning and I were not doll-playing types unlike my younger sister who could spend the whole day playing with her dolls. Juaning and I went out to their big beautiful garden and hunted for dragonflies or watched birds as they drank from their big marble fountain. My father had already lectured me so long and often in the past about the correct treatment of birds, so we just watched them drinking and bathing or chasing one another. Sometimes I would draw little sketches of them on paper and keep those drawings as a souvenir of that time.

I taught Juaning how to climb a huge guava tree in their backyard, but guavas are not always in season so we climbed other fruit trees like the tamarind and the *camachili* trees. In May. the month of *Flores de Mayo*, we picked the *sampaguita* flowers and strung them into leis for the altar of our Blessed Mother.

While we were busy with our activities, Juaning's brother, Basiling and his friend Nanding tried shooting balls through a makeshift basket on top of the wall in a far corner of their huge yard. They never bothered us and we never even looked at them. At least, not until the time when Basiling's father bought him a brand new bicycle, which, to our great surprise, Basiling already knew how to ride. After a while, Nanding also came dragging a bicycle with him

"Well, well," we chorused, "and where are you two going?"

"Oh, around town for a breath of fresh air," answered Basiling trying to sound casual although the pride in their voices was quite obvious.

"Good! Then buy us something to eat from the market," I ordered.

"We're not stopping anywhere," protested Nanding. "We will only make *pasikat* and show off our new bikes."

"Oh how selfish of you!" shouted Juaning," I will tell Papa you are just showing off your bikes. Let's see what he will say."

"No, don't do that!" pleaded Basiling. "You know he doesn't want us to be showing off."

"I'm going to tell because that's what you're doing," Juaning could be relentless, "unless you teach us how to ride too."

It sounded like a bribe to me but I wasn't going to interfere. I really wanted to learn how to ride."

"Okay, but not right away. Maybe next week, if we have the time. And you have to wear something else, not those dresses you're wearing. You would look indecent!"

"No, of course not. We will wear our bloomers," I countered although even then, I was already wondering how on earth I could manage to get past my mother in that attire." In those times women wearing pants were frowned upon and considered "cheap", but for physical education classes girls, wore "bloomers" which was actually a loose split skirt gathered tight at the top of the knee. Both Juaning and I each had a pair of those since they were standard physical education uniforms in school.

After about a week of biking around town the boys were quite tired but very happy. One day, we were in the flower garden when Basiling came and suddenly asked, "Hey, you want to start learning how to ride a bicycle today?"

"Of course! Are you serious?"

Quicker than lightning we left the *sampaguita* flowers we were stringing, and ran up to change into our bloomers. In excited anticipation of this event I had brought my bloomers with me one day, telling my mother it was some snacks we were going to have later in the day.

Before he even started to teach us how to hold a bike Basiling gave a little sermon. "One thing that I want to make clear is that we **did not** force you to learn how to bike, is that clear? You **begged us** to teach you."

"Don't worry about that," we assured him. "We're not 'fraidy cats."

Since there was only one bike at the moment, Basiling was to teach one of us first. I won the toss-coin so he turned to me.

"Okay! Spread your legs and mount!"

He was surprised at how fast I followed his command.

His parents were often away in their farmhouse and only *Aling* Sepa, the cook and two housemaids remained at home. *Aling* Sepa was coming home from the market when she saw Basiling holding one side of the handle bar and leading me around carefully down their long driveway.

"*Susmariosep!*" she exclaimed "*Si señorita Sarah ay nagbibisikleta! Naku ano ang sasabihin ng señora pag nalaman yan?*"*

"Keep quiet!" screamed Basiling. "And keep your mouth shut. Do not say anything to my parents or I will not give you anymore Tagalog

---

*"*Jesus, Mary, Joseph! Miss Sarah is riding a bicycle. What will the Señora say when she gets to know about it?*"

magazines to read."

In a little while Nanding came and started teaching Juaning too.

We spent three whole days learning the art of riding a bike, stopping only for meals or snacks. In the evening my mother was quite surprised that I would go to sleep right after shower and supper.

For a month or so Juaning and I took turns at one bicycle and either Nanding or Basiling followed us to see that we did not get into any accidents. But our summer break was ending and we still did not feel safe riding without our escorts, so we left that problem for the following summer. Even in school, Juaning and I were so excited that we wrote each other about what we would do as soon as summer vacation came. With the next summer break, however, there was a bigger problem. How could we all go riding together when there were only two bicycles? Nanding's brother lent us his because he felt too old to be riding around town, but that came only to three. We still needed another one.

Suddenly I had a devious thought. My father's office was in the provincial government building which was quite far from the center of town where the Municipal Government building was. Inside it was the Post Office. *Papá* had an office messenger whose job was to get the mail to and from the Post Office on a bicycle. I remembered hearing my father saying he had bought Felipe, whom we called Ipe, a brand new bike, complete with a headlight and a horn. So off I went to *Papá*'s office to make a deal with Ipe. I would do the mail business for him early in the morning and on top of that, I would give him 25 centavos—quite a sum in those times—for snacks, and he would let me use his bicycle until 3:30 in the afternoon. But I told him that under no circumstances could he appear before my father during the time I had his bike. He was very happy, of course. He did not have to work, he got money, and on top of that, he could play checkers with the security guard. My father was so busy that as long as the mail was taken care of and his secretary had no complaints he kept working on more important matters.

So Juaning and I were free to ride around in the opposite side of town, far from where we lived. There were many interesting things in the town that we had not even heard about. We came to know about a haunted house which belonged to a family whose mother disappeared mysteriously and whose spirit, according to gossip, still went around the abandoned welling turning the lights on at midnight.

In one of the houses, we were told, there was a *mangkukulam,* a witch, whom the people avoided with great fear. They claimed that if she had a quarrel with anyone, she could make them sick by just pricking a magic doll she had, using magic pins. Her house looked very gloomy and when we passed it we would cross to the opposite side of the street and make the sign of the cross

One day, we decided to go to the railway station to see the 12:00 train pull in with all its passengers. The train was usually full and we enjoyed seeing who of the people in the town had gone to Manila and were now returning.

I was frantically riding furiously ahead of Juaning because it was almost time for the train to pull in. At a blind corner there suddenly shot out a *calesa,* also going full speed toward the station. I did not have time to brake and I ran smack into the horse, breaking the two long rods that held the horse to the cab. The poor *cochero* who earned his living driving passengers to and from the station was, of course, furious. In his great fright and anger he exclaimed aloud at me, "Now where in the world can you see two *señoritas* riding a bike around town?"

He went straight to my father's office, not too far away from there, to tell *Papá* about the accident caused by his daughter.

My father was livid with anger and surprise as he called his messenger to scold him for lending me his bike. Poor Ipe was visibly shaking, fearing the loss of his job. But my father did not fire him.

As punishment he was told to accompany the rig owner to the best shop where his vehicle could be fixed within two days. The cost was of no concern, as *Papá* would take care of the bill. To the poor man, *Papá* gave some money to tide him and his family over the two days he would not be able to work.

At home that night, I got a double sermon.

"Don't you know," my father said, "that poor man's means of livelihood is his rig?"

"And where in the world" said my mother, "can you find a girl riding a bike around town? You have been sent to a school to learn how to be a lady, and you spend your vacation time biking around like a boy!"

My father grounded me for a week during which I wore long-sleeved blouses to hide the bruises I got from the encounter.

"Why are you wearing those long sleeves when it is so hot?" asked my mother.

"I feel a little bit chilly," I lied.

"Ah, you must be coming down with the flu," she said, and forthwith got me two aspirin tablets to swallow.

"I will take them after lunch. You've told me so often that it is not good to take aspirin on an empty stomach," I reassured her, but as soon as her back was turned I threw them down the kitchen sink.

Juaning came to see me during my confinement and we spent the time stringing *sampaguita* flowers into leis to send to the church for the *Flores de Mayo* festival.

Fortunately, this punishment came on the third week of May so that wasn't bad since in a week's time, we would be preparing to return to school which started on the first week of June. Somehow I felt that my father was not too greatly disappointed about my riding a bike because it was, for him, like having a son.

The following summer *Papá* was jubilant because I got all the gold medals in my class despite the big complaint that I still was not behaving like a genteel young lady. So, as a sort of a prize for my good grades he bought me a beautiful bike with a horn, a headlight, and special brakes. Not to be outdone, Juaning's parents also bought her one exactly like mine.

But this gift came with a special set of rules, one of which was that we must never, but never, go the area of the Laguna Lake where there were supposedly many notorious hoodlums and criminals. Furthermore, we were to be home before dark, five o'clock at the latest.

We felt like two turtles thrown into the water. Juaning's parents even ordered for both of us two pretty riding pants in different pastel colors that were really were very feminine. My father felt that we were just too far ahead of our times. But my mother was not completely happy. She just kept quiet and I'm sure prayed hard for our safety.

Santa Cruz was a fairly big town composed of several barrios or districts. Juaning and I visited the many outlying barrios and learned about the many people we never thought existed in the town. We were even invited to their harvest *fiestas* and their country style weddings with all their traditional trimmings and superstitions. In one of the barrios we came to know about the existence of another *mangkukulam* who could cure illnesses if she liked the people, or destroy those whom she didn't like with her voodoo antics.

At another place a huge *balete* tree trunk that lay almost horizontal to the ground with a great gaping hole was, according to the people in the neighborhood, the home of a big *cafre,* a giant, fearful-looking spirit who was the owner of the tree. We were told that when the tree bore fruit in summer anyone who wanted some fruit had to ask permission first. A loud groan meant that the *cafre* was not willing to grant the request, but loud laughter meant that he did. If people went against his wish, they would become very ill.

Juaning and I were like a couple of investigative travelers who learned many things that were quite new to us. Soon, though we had become bored with going to the same places day after day and were thinking of some other place to go that would be different from our daily rounds.

"Let's try going to Pagsangjan," I told Juaning one day.

"What?" she asked, surprised and a bit fearful. "You mean go out of town?"

" Yes, why not?" I countered.

Pagsangjan is a beautiful little town about 15 kilometers from Santa Cruz, which at that time, had preserved many of the fantastic Spanish features of a by-gone era. On the main street was an impressive row of mansions built along the florid architecture of the Castilian regime. Even the church in the very center of town had preserved its Iberian heritage. There were shops galore, in imitation of Manila. The people were mostly of European ancestry and according to some people, a bit snooty. Besides that, Pagsangjan also had beautiful waterfalls where people were fond of picnicking.

So one sunny day Juaning and I ventured out of Santa Cruz—without the permission of our parents. They would have been worried sick knowing there were railroad tracks to cross on the way there. It was a very lovely trip. We did not get too tired and we had lunch at one of the swanky restaurants with Juaning picking up the bill from her parents' house allowance during their absence.

"We must come here again!" I said." I will treat next time."

And so we did about a dozen more times, sometimes coming home for lunch when we had run out of money, or sometimes bringing food from the family kitchen leftovers.

Then one day close to the end of May, when we were as broke as church mice, Juaning suggested: "Let's go there but come back for lunch and eat at home. We'll be going back to school soon and we might not get the chance again."

"That's a very good idea," I approved happily.

So we biked again to the dear old town that to us had become sort of like a place of pilgrimage. We biked to the near and beautiful Pagsangjan Falls to say goodbye to it and made a wish that we could go back there again the following summer.

Then Juaning looked at her watch and exclaimed, "*Aba naku!*\* It is almost noon and I am a little hungry"

We hurried to the highway toward Santa Cruz. But upon reaching the railway crossing, we found a big crowd milling excitedly around because there had been an accident and the crossing was closed to traffic.

"*Dios mío!*"\*\* said Juaning, "What shall we do? We do not have a centavo to our name."

I approached the guard who was watching the crossing and he looked at us from head to foot as if we were two imps.

"No crossing," he shouted. "even the mayor cannot go through!"

"Suppose we just go on foot dragging our bikes?" I asked.

"*Aba!* These tomboys! You sure are pigheaded! I already told you NO CROSSING!"

Juaning began to cry.

"Don't cry," I comforted her. "Let's go back to town."

The only family I knew well enough in the town to ask for a meal was Dr. Llamas, father of Carlos P. Romulo's first wife Virginia, and my father's *compadre*. I had been at his house several times when they had parties and I was sure he would not have minded giving us lunch.

When he opened the door and saw us, he was genuinely surprised. "How did you get here?" he asked.

"We came on bicycles, sir," I explained lamely, "but we cannot go home because we cannot cross the railroad tracks. There was an

---

\* *My goodness!*
\*\* *My God!*

accident."

"You came on bicycles? From Santa Cruz?" He was incredulous.

"Yes sir, and we are very hungry and we do not have any money so we couldn't buy any lunch."

"Come in, of course you shall have lunch. And I shall call my *compadre*. He must be worried."

"He does not know we are here, sir," I remonstrated.

"Well he should know. My goodness! I thought you were studying to be a *señorita*. *Naku!* I have a joke on him!" He laughed loud and long.

As he spoke with my father while we ate, I heard him ask, "*Compadre*, is your child a girl or a boy? But don't worry, I'll have my driver accompany them to the railroad tracks and see that they get through."

Once we got home, we faced another lengthy sermon from the two sets of parents.

**T**hat was the last memorable summer adventure we had because in later years my father saw to it that we went to Baguio City, a popular destination for many lowlanders. It was up in the mountains, so cool and restful, and even before anyone reached the city itself, the fragrance of the pine trees already made us look forward to the vacation in the City of Pines. In the months of April and May my mother would drag us to Antipolo for the yearly pilgrimage to the Virgin of Safe Voyage. Usually, that's how my summers ended.

Now that I look back on it, I continue to feel that those were the most enjoyable, most carefree times in my life.

## *Chapter Four*

When I returned to the *Centro* after that memorable summer, there were more responsibilities as we were now in high school. We were no longer *pequeñas*, but *medianas* whose behavior was brought up as an example before the little ones. That in itself was a big responsibility since the little ones always imitated their older sisters. Even our schoolwork required more attention and study. But, as it was in grade school, my academic performance resulted in gold medals in all my subjects. Come to think of it now, I really do not remember having to spend too much extra effort in accomplishing that. Maybe I was just lucky to have studied for the questions that were asked in the exams. Even when I was still in my first year of high school, my teachers had already begun to speculate that I might be a good candidate for the *Excelencia* honor, the special award which was the equivalent to Valedictorian in other schools. But to receive that award one had to consistently rank first throughout high school. Academically, there did not appear to be any problems. If anything would keep me from getting the award, however, it was the matter of my conduct.

The first time I came to the *Centro,* as a little girl, we were shown the different uniforms that were on display. What held my attention was the *terno,* the festive costume of the women in the country. It had an ankle-length skirt with a short train pinned at the side. A blouse of fine pineapple apple fiber starched stiff with butterfly sleeves completed the costume. On its sleeves was the school logo with the words, *Ciencia y Virtud*— science and virtue—neatly embroidered in silver letters. I remember then, that when I saw that costume, I promised myself that someday I would wear it with pride and I knew how pleased my father would be if that happened.

So, when my teachers encouraged me to aim for the *Excelencia* award, I knew I could do it as far as my studies were concerned, but how could I change myself from being me? I did not seem to be getting any closer to becoming the sweet, genteel *señorita* that was expected of me and that was the hope of my father. Perhaps I just wasn't cut out for that role. I continued to be punished for running up and down the stairs and taking them two steps at a time. At times, especially when I knew I was being watched, I would force myself to walk demurely up or down the stairs, but it was not easy. My nature prompted me to move freely...to climb trees, to run, jump, and skip...to take two steps at a time...an expression of being me, of being free, of being myself.

*I*n my first year of high school, there was a big fire, followed by a series of small ones around the vicinity of the *Centro*. Fortunately, none of them affected us, but eight months later, the *Directora* decided we should go through a series of fire drills and be prepared in the event of a fire...heaven forbid! *Doña* Librada thought that we should learn to use the fire escape, evacuate the buildings in a disciplined way, and without any panic. Going through the drills would teach us to move faster. Thus, for three successive Saturdays, officers from the Manila Fire Department put us through fire drills and taught us safety behavior. We were shown how to position ourselves at the entrance to the fire escape and go down the ladder, stepping carefully, without panic, until we reached the last rung. Most of the girls were afraid and did not want to even try, but quite a few daring ones—among them myself—were willing to experiment. We practiced doing it several times and very soon we were familiar with the process of going up and down.

The *Directora* praised us loudly in front of all the other girls and said that if there should be another fire, we would lead all the groups of students. My friend, Lily, soon became an expert in going up and down the fire escape. I came in a pretty close second.

Two or three times during our evening prayers, we knelt beside the door that led to the fire escape, which was right opposite the dorm altar. We opened the door noiselessly and went up and down the fire escape without anyone noticing. It was very exciting and besides, there was a weird sense of devilish triumph for having escaped the eye of the strict *Maestra* Felisa.

Then one night, when we did not exactly enjoy the food we had for dinner, Tere, our pet name for Teresa Ilusorio whose bed was next to mine, said, "How nice it would be if we could just go out and eat at the Chinese restaurant two blocks away from here." We all gasped at the implication, but we all agreed it could be done.

"Why not?" exclaimed Lily. I could go down and get an order each of *pancit canton* and *camaron rebosado* and we could eat under Tere's bed."

Lily was only a half-boarder, but sometimes her parents left her in the dorm for a day or two when they went out of town. She knew that part of town very well and she did not care much about the discipline that *internas* were put through. So out she went, bought the Chinese dinner and we had a banquet under Tere's bed. No one else besides us knew any better and that became the first of many nights.

One moonlit night we were once again hungry for something to eat that was different from the usual fare. This time, however, we did not have Lily to do it for us.

With the prompting only of my true self, I said, "I'll do it!"

"No, no, no!" my friends chorused. "Remember, you are in the first year of high school now, and your conduct is being watched by all the teachers and officers. Whatever mischief you are caught doing will be recorded and checked against your qualification for the highest honor, the *Excelencia* Award."

"Who cares about that lousy award?" I said, and down I went to get the precious Chinese dinner. Lady Luck, most unfortunately, was not with me that evening, for as I came to the last rung of the ladder on my way up the fire escape, who should I see but the *sub-directora*, the Dean of Discipline of the school, waiting at the top of the ladder, right by the door of the fire escape.

At that very moment I lost everything—my dignity, my supper, which I was dreaming of enjoying that evening, and my chance at being a candidate for the *Excelencia* award. I felt sad and mortified because my father whom I loved so much and who was already so proud of me would be very disappointed. I knew he was hoping I would get honors when I finished high school. From that time on I vowed to myself that I would get all the gold medals in every subject of every year until my graduation.

First, however, let me explain the medal system at the *Centro*. Since its foundation, the school conducted an examination in each subject for all those who, from their class averages, would have been exempted from the tests. That way they could determine who should get the gold, the silver and the bronze medals for a particular subject.

I really studied very hard and prayed so that I could fulfill the vow I had made to myself. By my own kind of reasoning, if I got all the gold medals how could anyone be *Excelencia* with only silver and bronze medals, no matter what her conduct might be. Besides, something else was pulling in my favor. A change of policy by the Academic Board ruled that participation in extra-curricular activities and the study of foreign languages could compensate and outweigh a record of poor conduct, provided no crime punishable by law was involved. So, I enrolled in French classes for three consecutive years, following my father's suggestion. The *Directora,* wanting me to make up for my mistakes, enrolled me in Spanish Literature and Poetry under Don Manuel Ravago, Sr. That was how I got my rudiments of French and excellent polish in the Spanish tongue.

Besides that, during my second year in high school, Mr. Francisco Buencamino, my piano teacher, organized a *rondalla*—a five-piece band of strings and percussion instruments—and got the musically-inclined students to join. We could choose the instruments we wanted from the *banduria,* the *mandolina,* the *laud,* the Spanish guitar, or the *marimba.* The last one is similar to the xylophone but with bigger and longer tubes that gave it a sound similar to an organ. Nobody wanted this instrument so I chose it and later on was joined by my friend, Esperanza Nadres. The two of us became the first women marimbists in the country. Mr. Jose Silos, a well-known Filipino musician and a veteran trainer of *rondallas* rehearsed us almost every night and after some months we were good enough for public performances. The *Directora* was so proud of us that she made us play at a big program celebrating the birthday of Don Manuel L. Quezon, then President of the Senate.

We were a hit wherever we played and I was sure this would, in a way, compensate for and outweigh my poor conduct record. Besides with so many rehearsals, I didn't have the time to even think of creating mischief. I could not consider my piano and my ballet lessons since I had already been taking them way before my colossal misdemeanor. As the last three years of high school rolled by—years that were replete with great artistic activities like concerts, plays, dance presentations, and dramatic readings in English and Spanish—I was more and more assured of being listed among the candidates for the *Excelencia* Award.

However, as graduation day came nearer I could not help but feel sad. I knew I would be going home for the last time and not come back. After high school graduation, there would no longer be any reason for me to return to the *Centro.* I would leave all that I had loved and cherished for ten years of my life—my friends, my teachers, *Maestra* Felisa who was my mother for ten months of every year; *Maestra* Osang, who always corrected my table manners, *Maestra* Conching, who taught me Government and History. There was also *Don* Alberto Campos who taught me Spanish songs when I was very young and later was my teacher in Physics and Chemistry. And how could I ever forget *Señor* Buencamino, my piano teacher for eight years, and *Doña* Pilar who kept the keys to the front door and whom we had nicknamed Santa Petra. Lastly, the two women at the helm of the school, *Doña* Carmen de Luna, *sub-directora*, who punished and scolded us in the makeover that would turn us into refined ladies, and *Doña* Librada Avelino, my guardian angel for ten years whom I had learned to respect and esteem beyond words.

As it turned out, Fate—and hard work—made my dream a reality.

When the announcement was made that I would be given the *Excelencia* award, friends came to hug and congratulate me. I was exceedingly proud, of course, but I was also overcome with emotion and started weeping profusely, as if I had lost a dear relative.

"Tears of joy" everyone said, but for me, these were tears of genuine sorrow for I was closing what perhaps was to be the most innocent and beautiful chapter of my life. The only ray of happiness that lit up the darkness in my heart was the thought that I had made my father very happy and proud of me.

On graduation night, dressed most uncomfortably in a gorgeous, elegant terno bearing the college logo, created by the then most modern couturier, *Doña* Pacita Longos, and wearing all the family jewels—to please my mother—I walked on the arm of *Don* Josue Soncuya, one of the founders of the school. Slowly, he guided me from the back of the audience to the magnificent stage of the Manila Opera House. There, kneeling on a velvet cushion in front of the *Directora*, I was crowned with a wreath of golden laurel leaves, the symbol of knowledge and honor.

I heard thunderous applause and glancing at my father standing behind me in elegant formal attire, I was certain that his heart was swelling with pride over this mischievous little brat of his. After all his efforts of getting me to become the ideal that he had planned me to be from childhood, he had achieved his goal. It shone in his face as he came and hugged me on that triumphant night.

Later on I begged him to let me take my basic college courses at the *Centro* again, but he emphatically refused. "No, no, but no!" he said emphatically. "This time I want you to know that the world is not made up of women only. You are going to the University of the Philippines."

I knew him well enough by then and trusted his judgment especially when it had to do with my schooling, so I posed no arguments. When it came to his plans for me, *Papá* had always been right.

That was March, 1925. I was seventeen, ten months short of my 18th birthday when *Papá* planned to give a coming-out party for me. Always the practical one, with my graduation and especially because I had been given the *Excelencia* award, he decided to combine both parties—graduation and coming-out—into one. The venue would be the large Burnham Park Auditorium in Baguio City, where the national government held its summer sessions and where Manila's elite always retired for the summer. Baguio, the City of Pines, as it was called, was cool and hilly. The air was pure and fresh unlike Manila, always hot and humid during the summer months. It was the ideal place for a summer event especially since most of our family and friends would also be up in Baguio

*Papá* had managed to get a summerhouse in the City's Government Center where houses were available for government officials and their families. Besides our family of four, my father invited *Mamá's* only brother and his family to stay with us for they were in charge of my graduation cum coming out party. Poying, my cousin, was the manager and in charge of the whole affair. She had offered to do this for me and I trusted her since she was always my fairy godmother during my time at *Centro Escolar* where she also went to school. Helping her with the preparations were Meneling and Pepito, my playmates during the early years. Poying's eldest brother, Irineo, already a distinguished dentist and supreme authority on matters concerning the clan's teeth, thought that all this excitement over the party was rather silly. I still remember being thankful for all the preparations but not altogether happy because I knew that in two months I would no longer be returning to the *Centro,* my home for ten years. I would miss my friends, my teachers and all those places especially during the summer, where I had spent hours and hours of childish joys and learned in the process how to act like a lady.

There were many guests at my graduation-debut party, some of them driving up to Baguio only to attend it. I smile with a tinge of childish guilt at the recollection of an almost middle-aged Spanish writer and poet who dedicated verses about my "beauty" and "sweetness"— vivid descriptions using words that sounded more beautiful than the reality behind them—who came with a giant bouquet of Baguio red roses. My father had warned me to be very polite toward him, and so I was, though with much effort on my part. There he was, fifteen years my senior, already losing his hair, reciting love-poems in Spanish. My cousin, Meneling, whom I loved as my own brother, kept an eye on me and made sure that I was behaving correctly toward him. As I write this I really wonder what became of that Spanish dreamer.

My father and I opened the dance with the orchestra playing "Let me call you sweetheart." *Papá* was a fairly good dancer, but after a little while he handed me over to my friend, Tony Gonzales. From thereon, it was one dance after another with occasional visits to the buffet table. The party lasted until 10:30 P.M., an early night in today's terms but this was in the 1920s.

On the last day of April we left Baguio and drove straight to Antipolo, May, being the festive month of Our Lady of Good Voyage. I suppose, starting life on a new phase was something *Mamá* felt was a voyage for which I needed prayers and a send-off. She had rented a house that was much bigger than we needed because she knew that many of our relatives would be going there for one or two days to attend the procession or spend a week-end. My father was temporarily assigned in the Department of Finance for he was chosen by then President of the Senate Manuel L. Quezon to attend to the financial structure of the new Quezon City. Only my mother, my sister, and I remained in Antipolo. In thanksgiving for my successful graduation from high school and the new voyage I was about to embark on, *Mamá* financed a High Mass on a Sunday and a procession in the evening.

Life in Antipolo was very different from that of Baguio City. For the parade, the women and even the teen-aged girls wore the *balintawak,* a national costume that consisted of a colorful ankle-length skirt bound at the waist by a two-feet wide strip of harmonizing color called the *tapis*. The blouse was of the same crisp material, with butterfly sleeves that worn with the *terno* on festive occasions but instead of the *pañuelo* there was a strip of folded square cloth of the same material and design as the *tapis* worn over one shoulder. It was a very fetching sight to see a group of women dressed like this attending Mass or walking in the procession. My mother ordered six sets of those for me, but I was not really comfortable in them. She never stopped reminding me that I was no longer a bike-riding youngster but a budding young woman. We usually stayed in Antipolo for three weeks but this time, we cut it short as I had to prepare for school in Manila.

One person I really missed was my dear friend, Juaning and our daily meetings wandering near and far on our bicycles, getting into all kinds of scrapes and adventures, but also seeing places of scenic beauty like the Pagsangjan Falls. I had started to see less and less of her because somehow our interests had become different. She was going to take a Home Economics Course at the Philippine Women's College and I would be going to the University of the Philippines. Also it was the year that Juaning was the *Rosa Mística,* the Queen, of the *Flores de Mayo* festival and she had to prepare for that role. Another reason why I did not pursue our friendship further—which I never told any one—was that I heard from some of my mother's friends that Juaning's parents were grooming Basiling, Juaning's brother, to be my future husband. That got me really mad and I was sure my father would have been angry too had he known. Basiling was a good boy and I liked him like an older brother too because of my friendship with Juaning. After all, it was he who taught me how to bike. But nobody—and I repeat, nobody—would ever have to tell me when and whom I should marry.

## Chapter Five

After a week of preparations in June of that year, I found myself at the University of the Philippines. As proud as I was to be a college student—with all that the identity carried with it of pride, maturity, freedom—I found myself confused, even a bit scared at the beginning, not to mention mentally unprepared. It was so unlike the familiarity that bolstered my confidence every time I returned to the *Centro Escolar de Señoritas*, where everything was in place and so well ordered. At the UP, I had to get to know where the buildings were, and where my classes were going to be held. Registration alone was a frantic attempt at finding out what subjects I would be taking, where I would have to go for them and when. It's a good thing that in that crowd of freshmen as green as I was, my cousins were there to hold my hand and guide me through the process of being a college freshman.

One thing I did welcome was being in a classroom that would not be filled with only girls. Private Schools in the Philippines then were such that girls never went to the same school as boys. UP would be my first experience in a co-educational setting, something that I welcomed, since I had always been comfortable with the opposite sex. After all, my first playmates were boys, most of my cousins were boys and many of my summers were spent outdoors playing their games. The all-girls atmosphere at the *Centro,* was something I had to learn and become accustomed to and while I had come to be comfortable with that, it was the male-female companionship that was natural to me as I learned to climb trees, run through the fields, and race my playmates to see who could get the ripest mangoes. I saw that many of the female freshmen, who had grown up in all-girl schools like me, found themselves acting awkwardly around the boys...but not for long, I might add. Once the inhibitions imposed by our upbringing were overcome by the natural tendencies that come with adulthood, the awkwardness disappeared.

I quickly found myself in a "gang"—mostly young men—as *Papá* later on referred to them. A year in college together had made us close friends and I felt comfortable and safe in their company. They looked after my interests and would warn me to stay away from young men whom they felt I should not get close too. "Friendships are all right," they would say, "but there are certain 'types' you don't want to get mixed up with." They treated me as a younger sister and even called me "Baby" and I felt that these relationships were, all in the family. Their parents were friends of my parents and it was not as if we were getting to know each other for the very first time. Meneling, my cousin, was especially protective of me and it was to him that I would run to if I had a problem.

I did get to meet someone outside the gang, however. I met him for the first time when we took our entrance exams before we even enrolled. It was customary at that time, for all valedictorians and salutatorians to take a different exam from the regular graduates. We were assigned seats alphabetically. His name was Romeo Ledesma and my last name was Kabigting, so he sat on my right. Since he was enrolled in Engineering, I did not get to see him again for weeks until all the freshmen were invited to the Acquaintance Party and we talked for a while. The following semester when we compared schedules, he laughingly pointed out that we had a common vacant period at 3:30 on Wednesdays.

I was surprised to see him at the library the following Wednesday and somehow I sensed that he was there to see me. "How did you know I was here?" I asked. He smiled and told me that he knew I spent most of my free time in the library. So he decided to wander over to see whether his instincts were right. From thereon, we always met at the library whenever either one of us could make it. He always got there first and reserved three vacant seats at a table in a corner near the window. The other chair was reserved just in case I brought someone else along with me.

We really did study, at least that first year. But this companionship abruptly ended as I found myself occupied with an activity that would determine my career later on in life, although at that time, I had no idea of this.

Towards the end of that year, Mr. Verne Dyson, my English professor, encouraged me to try out for a role in the UP Day presentation. It was a play called *Grandma Pulls the Strings*.

During my ten years at the *Centro*, I had already acted in plays. Typically in girls' schools, however, girls played all the roles, even when the characters called for happened to be male roles. Having had some experience and interested in doing something different, I promised Prof. Dyson I would go and see if I could land a role. After tryouts, my name was listed down for the role of the little girl in the play, and I was told to watch the Bulletin Board for the announcement of those chosen for the cast. After looking at the board daily for about a week, I found my name among those chosen, although the cast was still tentative. Thrilled by the possibility of being in a play with a mixed cast, I immediately went to the office of Dr. Fansler, Head of the English Department, who referred me to Mrs. Fansler who was directing the play. According to Mrs. Fansler, I was cut out for the role of the thirteen-year-old girl who came out with smart lines in the play. It must have been my diminutive size and my natural ease with smart comebacks. So I studied the role as best as I could and was determined to make my performance a success.

For the UP Day celebration I was also in a folk dance contributed by the Department of Physical Education. It was an old, elegant Spanish group dance called *Lanceros* in which the women wore voluminous skirts of velvet, with a *camisa* of starched Brussels lace embroidered with gold and silver threads and decorated with scattered beads. I do not believe it was my singular grace and poise in carrying out the intricate steps of the dance that got me chosen. There were only a few of us who could afford the seventy-five pesos for the costume, but my father was very willing to pay just to see me float around in something so elegantly feminine.

The summer after my freshman year, *Papá* invited my men-friends at the UP to spend Easter with us in Baguio. He was very happy to see how we related to each other in the group and was relieved that the days when I used to fight with my playmates seemed to be a thing of the past. Among those who came were Nicanor Hidalgo, Gilbert Romulo, the younger brother of Carlos P., Joe Rodas, Peping Mendoza, Danding Romualdez, Gil Puyat, and Pepito Gutierrez. Those whose families had residences in Baguio stayed with them, but the others stayed with us.

It was a grand vacation. We went to the Trinidad Valley where the Igorots—natives of the Mountain Province—had many big gardens grown with all kinds of vegetables. They looked so temptingly fresh that we bought some to bring home for *Mamá* to make a meal for us. We also went to the City Market and brought home colorful clothes and linens woven by the mountain folk. We hiked up and down hills and visited the cave where the skeletons of about a dozen people were seated in a circle as if they were holding a meeting. A warning was written on a piece of wood in English: "Do not touch any of the skeletons or you will have bad luck." I remember that Joe Rodas did not believe in the warning and he took a pipe from the hand of one of the skeletons, planning to take it home as a souvenir. On the way home, he fell into a ravine and broke his ankle. The Red Cross had to be called and he was taken to a hospital. The pipe was, of course, returned to its rightful owner. Our vacation ended with a ball at the Burnham Park Auditorium on the evening of Easter. That was the crowning activity of a pleasant and memorable vacation.

In my second year of college, I had an additional interest. Eugenia Guidote taught me the breaststroke. I liked it much better than the Australian crawl, which for some reason made me swallow water with every breath. Swimming the breaststroke kept the body in rhythmic graceful movements and allowed full-lung breathing periods. I was really so happy with my newly acquired prowess that besides the required classes in swimming, I was in the pool every afternoon.

It was also about that time that I had a class in American Literature from 4:30 to 5:30 under Professor Romulo. On Wednesdays, I had a class immediately after that at the swimming pool, which was a big block away on the Isaac Peral side of campus. Professor Romulo had allowed me to leave at the first bell, with Danding, who was in the same class, trailing behind me. Professor Geronimo Suva had warned me that I had already been late for swimming class twice and the third time would be considered an absence. He was stern and I knew he meant it. He even went around and touched the students on their shoulders to see whether they had already showered. To help me save on minutes, Poying, my cousin who always played "fairy godmother" to me even when we were still at the Centro, came up with a solution. She made me a dress that zipped all the way up in front. All I had to do was unzip and wriggle out of it since I was already wearing my swimsuit. After getting rid of my shoes and dress, which Danding, who ran along with me from class, so considerately, put away in a bag, I could get into the shower on the run and jump into the pool. Danding was an absolute dear to do this for me once a week. Then, he would sit by the door of the pool and after I was done, we would go to the corner store and have some halo halo for 25 centavos a cup.

This went on without a hitch for several weeks until one day, I saw my name on the Bulletin board of the Dean of Women calling me in for an interview. The following day, I went to her office. Our Dean of

Women at that time was a not-so-young-anymore spinster who was very strict about campus morals. As soon as I came in, I knew I was in for it. She glared at me and said: "Miss Kabigting, it has been reported to this office that you were undressing while crossing the campus. And, to make it worse, you did that while the ROTC cadets were drilling. What have you to say for yourself?"

Her tone of voice made me indignant and I said: "First of all, I was NOT undressing, ma'am. I was changing my outfit without undressing. I already had my swimming suit underneath my zip-up dress and all I did was bring the zipper down to my waist."

"The swim-suit is not decent enough to be a dress."

"If that is the case, then why is it the prescribed wear for swimming? In less than five minutes, I would be in the swimming pool. If the swim suit is not decent enough to be a dress, then all the women in the swimming class are in indecent attire."

"I do not want to discuss this any further. You are getting ten points of discipline. You may go now."

I was so angry that I was seeing red. When Danding heard about it, he quietly reproached me. "You know, you could have chosen the other American Literature class at 3:30, and not have to make a run for your swimming class, but, of course, you had to take the one under Professor Romulo. So this is what you get."

"Oh, no!" I retorted. "I am not going to take this sitting down. Do you know that every point of discipline is equivalent to three hours of Physical Education? NO! I'm not going to take this."

And with that, I went straight to the President's office. Upon hearing my story, the President immediately called his secretary to call the Dean of Women for a conference. I was told to go and I would be informed about the results of their talk. I told him that if she did not cancel the 10 points she gave me, I would go to the Student Council and make a precedent of this case. I would also publish my complaints in the *Philippine Collegian*, the campus newsletter.

Three days later, I saw my name on the President's Bulletin board. When I went in to see him, he was all smiles and welcomed me in.

"*Hija*, I got the opinions of four deans on the matter and they were all on your side. Your 10 points have been cancelled."

I thanked him and apologized for all the trouble.

"You see!" I told Danding, "I had to claim my rights. I felt it was unfair and I had to speak my mind." As my father had often said, *"El que no llora, no mama."*\*

So I went on with my swimming. In addition to the breast stroke, Eugenia, whose nickname was Gening, and her sister, Munding, taught me some life-saving techniques using the frog-kick. I became so good at it that my name was included in the swimming guards list and was among those assigned to watch the swimming classes. We were paid fifty centavos an hour and each of us stayed three to four hours at a time.

My cousin, Meneleo Carlos, who was already teaching at the College of Engineering and was through by 3:30 P.M., had to wait for me until 5:00, which was when I was done. He patiently waited for me knowing how happy I was with the job. I loved this activity so much that it kept me from trying out for several plays that were shown in preparation for the UP Foundation Day Celebration.

It was in that same year that I went through a lot of emotional stress. Romeo Ledesma and I had started to become quite close. I saw him as my "special friend"...one might say, I had started to think of him as my first love. The boys in my gang were my brothers, my playmates who had helped me adjust to college life. The meetings Romeo and I had at the library the year before went continued. Most of the time, he would

---

\**The baby that does not cry, does no get to suckle.*

hold my hand under the table while I was reading, and when, I had to write, he would just sit there and once in a while, touch my cheek. I felt I was falling in love with him. In the caressing Visayan dialect, he asked if he could call me *hamut* which in Visayan means "sweet smelling."

Meneling was the first to notice that it was Roming who often took me to the parking lot of the Department of Engineering where he always left his car. On days when it was Danding who brought me home, I was always with him at the porch of the UP Hall building.

One day, Danding asked me on our way home, "Are you in love with Roming?"

"I don't know, but I feel good when he talks to me and holds my hand, and when he calls me *hamut*," I answered.

"Maybe you are in love, and it is the first time you feel like this. But do be careful. Just don't do anything foolish that you might regret later," he advised.

Meneling also noticed and asked me point blank, "Has he kissed you at any time?"

"Ladies do not kiss and tell," I answered

"Well, if he has kissed you, do not let it go beyond that. Remember, you promised your father you would not think of marriage until after you finished college."

It bothered me that Meneling and Danding had started to ask questions even though I knew they were only trying to be protective. But perhaps that was the problem. I wasn't so sure that I wanted to be protected.

We never did go beyond the behavioral bounds that were the order of the day. Thinking back on it now, I believe Roming and I were two very young amateurs getting the natural urge for someone special to love. We were both trained from childhood in non-coeducational schools where information with regard to sexual attraction was never given, let alone mentioned. Most of the time, we put down our feelings in notes that we exchanged every single day since we could not talk much in the library. He was a very expressive writer and he put all his ardent feelings in a language that was florid and touching. For my part, saturated as I was with the consuming passion of Spanish literature, I poured my heart out to him in heartfelt endearments for which the Spanish language knows no master.

During the first semester of our third year in college, he was called home. His father was sick and, as the eldest of three sons, he had to make the sacrifice of giving up college and taking over the family sugar holdings in Negros. I knew it was more the fear of his family that he might lose his head and jump into a hasty marriage with me, but this was only my intuition. When he came to say good-bye, he asked me to promise that I would not go to any party nor be friendly with any other man. He wanted me to wait for him until he came back. That sort of jarred me and I told him it was a crazy request because life might possibly take us in different directions and we had to live it as it came to us. I did go as far as to promise him that whatever happened to me, there would always be a place for him in my heart. And I kept that promise. He eventually married a prominent lady from their circle of friends in Negros and had two wonderful daughters. His family and mine were close and the young ones called us *Tito* and *Tita* just as though we were blood relatives. In 1961, when I came to Washington for my Fulbright Scholarship in Theater at the Catholic University, one of his daughters was already there and her family officially became my homefolk.

But that afternoon he left, I felt a big void in my heart, and it made me feel sad. I was very much at a loss, a feeling I had never felt before. Even Danding and Meneling noticed how quiet I was and tried very hard to cheer me up. My whole gang teased me. "Baby has lost her rattle!" they said, but very gently. I knew they were all concerned and I was grateful they were there for me through my first, deep, emotional loss. They were true friends and sure enough, with their help, and time, I eventually got over my first love. Besides, there was the daily grind of classes, homework, swimming and other activities that soon claimed most of my attention and energy.

Later on that year, Dean Jorge Bacobo's play about José Rizal, called *In 1898* was the big stage production. I knew that Gening was chosen for the principal role and often, I accompanied her to rehearsals. I had not tried out for any role because I preferred swimming to attending rehearsals and memorizing lines. I did help Gening to memorize her lines though. The play was about the marriage of José Rizal to Josephine Bracken before he was shot by a firing squad at the Luneta. I knew Gening would make a very pretty bride.

Ten days before the play, however, I found Gening in tears. She had come to the swimming pool area where I was doing somae guarding, saying that her boy friend, Gil Puyat, did not want her to wear a wedding gown in the play. Apparently, one of Gil's aunts had said there was a superstition where they came from that when a woman wore a wedding gown before she was married, the marriage would not take place. So Gil told her to make a choice—marriage to him, or the play.

"My goodness!" I exclaimed, unbelievingly. "Gil doesn't belong in the stone age. Why should he believe in such trash? It's only a play!"

"Well," Gening said between sobs. "Obviously he does because he gave me an ultimatum."

"But doesn't he realize that the show is only ten days away?" I found myself screaming at her. "Who will they get to take your place? At this late hour!" I was incredulous!

"That's part of the problem. Dean Bocobo is out of his wits trying to look for a substitute."

While we were talking, I heard my name being paged over the loud speaker, telling me to go to the office of the President.

"Now what have I done again?" I asked myself.

I went to the phone at the Physical Education office to let them know I was on my way to the President's office.

As soon as I got there, President Palma greeted me in Spanish.

"*Cómo estás, hija; me alegro de verte. Ven aquí y siéntate.*"*

"*Gracias, señor. ¿En qué puedo servirle?*"**

"Well, I am told that Gening Guidote is bowing out of the play."

"So I was told, sir."

"And the author, Dean Bocobo, tells me that the only one who can replace her at this late time is you."

"Me?" I wasn't aware that my voice had come out as a scream, I was so flabbergasted. "Sir, I'd never look the part of a bride. No one would ever believe me. I would never be able to look half as good as Gening can."

"But even Gening says you are the only one familiar with the lines because you have been rehearsing her.

"That part is true, sir, but I don't know the blocking at all. I would only wreck the play and I will go down in the history of the UP as someone who did something she knew she could not do."

"*Pero, hija*" he said, "There are still ten days left and that play is the highlight of the celebration. People will laugh at us if we do not present it. At least think about it, will you?"

"All right, I will think about it, sir. But I will also look for a substitute." And with that, I left President Palma's office.

That afternoon, Danding Romualdez and I had our Journalism I class under Professor Carlos Romulo, my teen-age idol. I remember how Danding never ceased to blame me for taking this section which was held on the 3rd floor of the Rizal Hall when we could have taken the

---

* "*How are you my child; I am happy to see you. Come and sit down.*"
** "*Thank you, sir. What can I do for you?*"

same class on the first floor of another building. My reason was that I wanted to have Professor Romulo as my teacher and he told me I was crazy. While we were going up the stairs to our class, Danding asked me what the President wanted and when I told him, he was surprised that I did not say "yes" right away to the request. I told him I'd said that because I was only second choice...someone who had to fill up an empty space.

"How can you say that?" he said, showing his disappointment in me.

"This is an emergency and they think only you can save the situation. You will be doing this for the UP."

"You're talking like President Palma," I said.

"That's the only way to talk about it," he retorted.

By then we were inside the classroom and there were many students so he kept quiet but I knew he was disappointed in me.

When Professor Romulo came, he stopped by my seat in the front row and said he would like to see me in his office after class. My heart sank because I was sure he would talk to me about the term paper I had handed in the week before, which I did not really prepare very well because I was at the pool most of the time.

As it turned out, I was wrong. He talked to me for a long time trying to convince me to take the role that Gening had left. He appealed to my common sense, my ability to take on challenge, my loyalty to the school. He argued so convincingly about doing something for the honor of the Alma Mater. How could I, a mere student, shut my ears against all that eloquence? In the end, I could not refuse. I just didn't know how I could. As I was about to leave, he patted my shoulder and said, "You will see! All UP will love you."

When I met up with Danding, who was waiting for me at the porch of Rizal Hall, he asked me what Professor Romulo had to say. I told him that I had just accepted the role of Josephine Bracken for the play. He looked at me and, shaking his head, he said, "Whatever hold he has on you, he certainly knows how to turn it on."

I worked hard, memorizing lines and pacing, practicing the blocking, often rehearsing until way past midnight. I also had to make trips to the dressmaker who had to alter the wedding gown made to Gening's measurements. I was smaller than Gening which was probably much easier for the dressmaker than if I had been taller. I wasn't sure I could pull it off so I prayed hard as well for success, considering I only had ten days of rehearsals.

Finally, the rehearsals were over. I stood in the wings waiting to make my entrance. Once on stage, I became Josephine Bracken. Overnight, I had become one of the most popular coeds on campus. Professor Romulo thanked me over and over and sent me a beautiful corsage of orchids after the play. To this day I cannot decide whether I was happier over my success, or the orchids, which I pressed and kept for a long time among my photos and souvenirs of college.

The summer after my third year in the UP, the university decided to offer several summer subjects in Baguio, and students who wanted to lighten their load for the coming school year could enroll in three subjects instead of only two as in the previous year. Our gang thought it was a great idea. We would enroll in two subjects in the morning and leave our afternoons free for fun.

A building was rented for the student dorms. The women would be housed on the upper floor with the famed super disciplinarian Miss Nieves Hidalgo as Dean of Women In charge of the men who would occupy the ground floor, were professors Clemente Uson and Nicolaas Zafra. There were twenty women on the upper floor and some male students and some professors with their families in the lower level.

Miss Hidalgo laid down the ground rules that, in no uncertain terms, would be followed to the letter. On weekdays the women could go out after classes leaving a note as to whether they would have lunch in or outside the premises. They could take the afternoon and evening off provided everyone was in before TEN THIRTY P.M. at which time the doors would be locked until morning.

In our group was Remedios Reyes, Nitang Molina, Alicia Palma, daughter of the UP President Rafael Palma, and I. Our friends in the lower floor were Joe Rodas, Gilbert Romulo, Peping Mendoza, and Pepito Gutierrez.

My father agreed to the idea of my enrolling for the summer there because he also had to be in Baguio in those days for the conference of the Department of Finance. Besides, the lady in charge of our dorm, Miss Hidalgo was a great friend of his.

In the first two weeks everything went fine. The lessons were not too heavily loaded with homework and by 3:30 in the afternoon, all classes were done. The students and professors went their own separate ways exploring the wonders of Baguio City. Our gang always went as a group to the market, to Trinidad Valley, and to the City Market. In the evenings, there were all kinds of happenings at the Burnham Park auditorium. There would be dances on Wednesdays and Fridays and on other days, some theater performances which would be announced later.

Our group wanted to go to the dances but the hours were a bit difficult for us. On Wednesdays the dances ended at nine-thirty, but the ones on Friday ended at 10:30 P.M. All of us wanted to dance up to the last musical beat, especially if it was the Philippine Constabulary Band which was playing. The problem was that the doors of our dorm would close at 10:30 and there was no way would make it on time.

So, one great mind among us, whom I can no longer recall came up with the suggestion that since Alicia Palma, who should not be dragged into any mischief because of her father's position, could be prevailed upon to at least perform the service of turning the hands of the huge clock at the door one hour back every Friday. We would then take care of turning it back correctly when we got in. It was quite an easy job since everyone especially Miss Hidalgo, whose room was farthest from the door, would be fast asleep.

Alice was not happy to do it but since she belonged to the group she said she would. And for the first two Fridays, we succeeded. We rested for one Friday and on the fourth Friday, when we were almost at the end of summer, someone in the dorm, after consulting her watch noticed that the clock was late one hour, so she quickly adjusted it.

When we got home the door was already locked. We did not know what to do. We toyed with the idea of just sitting there till morning until the door would open and give some lame excuse why we did not get home on time. But the boys in our group would not buy it. We would all get sick sitting there for eight or nine hours freezing in that cold temperature. They suggested that we go into the lower dorm where they could build a fireplace in the living room. We protested because Miss Hidalgo said at the beginning of the summer course that the men's area was absolutely off limits to the women, and the transgressor would be expelled from the UP.

When the boys saw we were not convinced, they went to Professor Zafra to explain the problem to him. The professor came out and said:

"I know I may lose my job for doing this but I feel it my Christian duty not to let you get sick waiting out there." And he opened the door to us.

So we went in. Mrs. Zafra gave us some cookies and lemonade and the boys spread some thick blankets on the living room floor. None of us could sleep because we feared the judgement that was to come to us in the morning.

Sure enough Miss Hidalgo was at the door when we lumbered in like a pack of convicts.

"I want to see all of you in my office after breakfast," she ordered imperiously.

Since it was a Saturday we did not have any classes. We had time to eat very slowly thinking about what we would say when we were questioned about the night before. We could not tell her we went into the men's dorm because she would not believe we just stayed in the living room. And the boys would be punished too. So we decided not to tell them anything, not even with the threat of expulsion hanging over our heads.

The first thing she did when we came to her office was just that.

"Where did you all spend the night?" she asked like an executioner.

Nobody answered. A pause and she repeated her question. Still no one made a sound.

"What is the matter," she roared, "have all of you suddenly turned dumb?"

Nobody answered.

"Then I will have to contact the Dean and recommend expulsion for the four of you." And she got up and went to the phone. Still, nobody said a word.

She talked with Dean Maximo Kalaw. From the little we heard, we surmised that the Dean was sending Assistant Dean Fonacier to Baguio that very day.

"I am more than ever convinced that you spent the night sinfully!" At this point we turned to look at one another. "So you cannot even mention what you did."

My father was informed about the case and he was deeply concerned. As soon as I saw him I cried because I could not tell him the whole truth.

Assistant Dean Fonacier whom I called Daddy Fonacier because he had helped me with my work since I was a freshman, talked to me privately before the investigation started.

"No matter how bad the case may be I want you to tell the whole truth and I will see how we can deal with it. You cannot just lose all you have worked for these years just like this. To be expelled from a university will give you a cruel stamp for the rest of your life and in everything you do."

The session opened with Miss Hidalgo as prosecutor. I was ready to tell the whole truth whether they believed me or not. I looked around and saw that Professor Zafra and his wife were present.

Before Dean Fonacier could open the investigation in the living room of the women's dorm, Professor Zafra asked that he be allowed to speak first regarding the case in question.

All of us—the accused—looked at one another, fearful of what he was going to say.

"Inasmuch as none of these young ladies want to say a word about their whereabouts last night," he began—to the great surprise of all—"I would like to give you the whole version since I was an active participant in it," he said.

All heads turned to him and there was an ominous silence.

"At about 11:00 P.M. last night I heard a group of students—four girls and four boys—discussing something near the door of the first floor dorm. I opened the door to see what it was all about and I was informed that the girls were locked out of their upper floor dorm. I did not have the heart to let them freeze waiting till morning outside for that would surely make them sick. So I asked them to come in. I led them to the living room near the fireplace and the boys brought out some blankets and pillows, laid them out on the floor and lit a glowing fire to warm the room. My wife stayed with them until they fell asleep. In the morning we gave them a very light breakfast of crackers and coffee. Now I know that the great problem is why they do not want to say anything about what they did last night. They are afraid that if they told the truth they would drag the boys in whatever punishment was due them. I am declaring this on my word of honor as a professor and in charge of the men's dorm, and I can cite Professor Uson and Professor Gohkale as my witnesses.

Everyone in the room heaved a great sigh of relief. Miss Hidalgo looked sheepishly at my father for it was she who told him that it was going to be no less than expulsion for this offense. My father was greatly relieved and happy because Assistant Dean Fonacier said that expulsion was out of the question.

Miss Hidalgo told us that she would like to see the four of us girls at her office at 3:30 that afternoon. Nitang, Medy, Pilar and I were expecting the worst from her as she was noted for being very narrow-minded in many things.

And sure enough when she came she read her decision as if she were reading a death sentence. We were to be in the dorm no later than 10:00 P.M. every night. To which all of us said "amen" happily. That seemed a very light sentence considering that we thought it would be a lot worse. Most of all, we were grateful that none of these involved Alicia Palma.

To sort of relieve the tension among the people concerned in the investigation my father invited everyone—the professors, the boys, Miss Hidalgo and her brood, meaning us—for the next day, which was a Sunday, to a party at the Pines Hotel. He also invited some friends of his who were staying at the hotel then, among them a tall handsome doctor, Jose Rodriguez who happened to still be a bachelor. As Fate would have it he was attracted to Miss Hidalgo as soon as he met her.

That very evening he issued a private invitation to only Miss Hidalgo and "her girls", meaning us, for a party at the Burnham Auditorium the next Friday which was a dance day. Our den mother accepted it graciously. We had a grand time as the boys of our gang were also there though not exactly with our group. On our way home at 10:30 P.M. Dr. Rodriguez took us first to an ice-cream parlor for some midnight snacks.

After that there were many more other occasions when we were invited by the kind doctor or by my father who found himself acting Cupid for our den mother and the eager suitor. Some evenings we went bowling or went to a movie and soon we realized to our happiness that our punishment had disappeared into thin air.

I do recall that some weeks after the Baguio summer course, Miss Hidalgo was married to Dr. Rodriguez with my father as the happiest guest of all. When my father became sick during the war Dr. Rodriguez treated him and never left him until he was positively cured. Such was the friendship that bound them. The last time I was able to see Mrs. Rodriguez, it was to admire their handsome young son who, I believe, was called Victor. Now whenever some friends refer to him as Dr. Rodriguez's son, I always quip: "That is the product of my father's playing cupid to his parents."

As Shakespeare said it so well: "All's well that ends well." And that episode in my life really did end very well.

## Chapter Six

My senior year in college was the most stressful of all my UP years, but I suppose this is generally true for every college student. While I had reduced my subject load by taking summer classes in Baguio there were still so many loose ends to tie up before I could be sure I would be graduating that year. There were term papers to submit, manuals to complete and hand in before the end of the first semester, make-up hours for physical education absences or tardiness, not to mention all my extra-curricular activities. I still had my swimming guard job and continued to love it, but I finally had to give it up when Professor Romulo, who was a publisher of four Manila newspapers collectively called DMHM, gave me a part-time job. I was appointed Spanish editor of the *Philippine Collegian*, and the UP student organ, and Professor Romulo also asked me to translate the society page of the Philippines Herald into Spanish for *El Debate*. The offices of the publications were in a building just walking distance away from the UP, so I walked there between classes to do the job. It paid me 75 pesos a month, and every time I received my salary, I gave the gang a treat at the corner store. I never told my father about this because I was afraid he would withdraw my monthly allowance of the same amount had he known I was earning that much. The job lasted only until my graduation in March of 1929.

All these would require my stay on campus until about five or six o'clock in the evening. I could not keep my cousin, Meneling, waiting for me after his classes in the College of Engineering were done at three in the afternoon. To remedy the situation *Papá* prevailed upon his friend, Mr. Felipe Ongkiko, a former resident of Santa Cruz Laguna where he had been assigned some years back, to let me stay in his home situated three blocks from the UP, for my last year in College. I was given a private room with a full bed and a big *armoire* and had the comfort and privacy that my father paid for handsomely and for which my mother sent loads of fruit and delicacies.

My work really kept me literally on my toes and oftentimes I complained to my gang about it to which they answered, "Never mind, this is the last lap, remember?" And we would all laugh.

In our Junior year, the gang got an addition to the group. Lourdes Paredes was a comely and very bright pre-law freshman. She was the daughter of Senator Quintin Paredes, Sr. and sister of Quintin Paredes, Jr. who was already studying in the College of Law. Lourdes, popularly known as Nenita, and I quickly became very close friends. We were assigned to the same group in Botany I, and our lockers were next to each other at the Physical Education Department. She often remarked that it was sad we had only one more year together as I was supposed to graduate in that year, but I always countered saying that our friendship did not have to end with graduation.

One afternoon while we were working on our Botany manuals she suddenly said "I have a good plan that will ensure our friendship forever."

"What's that?" I asked, surprised.

"You shall name your first daughter Lourdes after me. I shall be her godmother and you shall call her Nenita, like me," she said with aplomb.

"Wonderful!" I exclaimed, delighted, then laughing, I asked, "And if, I never get to have a daughter? Should I still call my boy Nenito?"

"That's just what you have to do," Danding Romualdez put in to tease her.

"You are a wonderful kibitzer," Nenita said, "But I will pray for a girl and you will see. It will happen. I do believe in the power of prayer."

"I am a witness to that," put in Joe Rodas who happened to be around.

Years later, my second birth gave me a girl, and Nenita lost no time in going to the hospital to tell the nurse in charge of records that the baby was to be named Lourdes.

My Senior year also found me in another play. The UP English Department decided to put on a full-length play, *East Lynne* that had to be very well rehearsed as it was the first foreign play the UP ever presented. The Director was Lt. George Kinney of the US Army who was not a faculty member. My role was the second lead, the leading man's mistress. Frances Bennet played the first lead, and Pete Syquia played the Lord. My role as mistress was the juicier part than that played by the wife. One of the beautiful scenes I remember was when I had to sing while crying. It was the first time I ever had to do that on stage. The director gave me special coaching sessions so that I could cry and still be understood. The Manila newspapers wrote rave reviews of the play and I was thrilled to have been given mention as a budding actress.

Early in my senior year, my friends at the UP discovered that I played the marimba when I invited them to a program at the *Centro Escolar de Señoritas* in celebration of the *Sub-Directora*, *Doña* Carmen de Luna's birthday. In representing the *Centro's* Alumnae Association, I played the marimba with my former co-marimbist, Esperanza Nadres.

Having found out, the UP lost no time in putting in a solo marimba number in the next UP program by the Women's Club. I told *Papá* about it and instead of bringing my marimba from Santa Cruz, Laguna, he rented one from the Lyric Music House, which had a shop at the Escolta, Manila's main shopping street at that time. My number was so well applauded that I had to do three encores. I suppose it was because I was one of the very first women marimbists in the country. I played again at the Seniors' Farewell Party in a duet with Quintin Paredes Jr.

When classes were resumed after the New Year in 1929, I saw in the office of the Philippine Collegian, the UP student newspaper, a copy of the tentative program for the coming UP Day celebration. I discovered that I was featured in it as a marimba soloist. My friends in the UP gave my name to the program committee of the celebration and they decided to include this as a novelty.

My first reaction was anger because I felt that I should at least have been asked before my name was included in the program. On second thought, however, and upon seeing the word "tentative" on the title page, I reconsidered thinking that the committee had probably meant to tell me before printing the final copy.

But I started to worry over the pieces that I should play. I had a pretty well rehearsed repertoire of only nine pieces, and it would be nice if I could get something more popular and more cheerful than the kundimans and the semi-classical pieces that my marimba teacher, Mr. Silos, had given me. Another reason was the fact that most of the pieces I knew were accompanied by a full orchestra or by a *rondalla*, a string ensemble. I was certain that would not have been possible for the UP program.

So I decided to go to the Lyric Music House on the Escolta, to look for something that could be accompanied by only a guitar or piano.

I asked Nitang Molina, a friend and classmate of mine to go with me.

"That's good," she said," we may meet the King of Jazz who works there,"

"And who is the King of Jazz?" I asked surprised.

"Are you still living in the past? You're probably the only one who hasn't yet heard of him, Ping Joaquin, the son of the popular lawyer, Leocadio Joaquin."

"Oh that one?" I remarked, not really interested. "So who made him King of Jazz?"

"His piano playing! He plays jazz on the piano like no one else. Do you know him?"

"Well, I used to see him now and then when I'd go to Tio Badong's house in Paco. You know after Mass on Sundays when people would gather outside the church ."

"We might see him this afternoon. He usually hangs out at the Lyric. So hurry!"

And sure enough, there he was, big as life, when we got there. As we came in, he was playing the piano in the midst of a small crowd around him listening to his rendition of some jazz piece which was the craze at that time.

Johnnie Raymundo, one of the brothers who ran the store, welcomed us with a big smile.

"Come in and listen to the King of Jazz," he said, thinking we had gone there for that purpose. "Thank you," I replied, "but actually we're here for something else."

"Oh fine, what can I do for you?"

"I am looking for some pieces for the marimba, something that could be accompanied by a piano or a guitar."

"Oh we have plenty of those. Come to the next room where the marimbas are and I'll get you the pieces. You can try them out while you choose."

We were ushered to the next room where a shiny new marimba invitingly sat in a corner. I went straight to it and played a very short piece, softly, so as not to disturb the jazz session going on in the front of the store. I remember now that I played the Visayan song, *Ay Kalisud*, a plea from a broken-hearted woman. The mellow tones of the marimba sounded like a lover in despair.

Suddenly the sound of the piano dishing out some perky jazz tune stopped completely and I saw the little crowd walking toward our room. And there was the piano player himself, walking to toward us.

I recall that I stopped and stood there as if I had been struck by lightning. I could not believe who I was looking at. Instead of the simple and timid teen-ager I used to see after Mass at the Catholic Church of Paco, standing before me was a strikingly handsome full-grown man walking gracefully toward me, his face lit up with a most disarming smile.

"How are you?" he asked me his hand stretched out to take mine. "I heard you play the marimba, but I did not know you could make it cry."

"Thank you," I said, trying to be gracious. "That's a beautiful compliment. But, I was merely trying the marimba because we may have to get one for the show next month. And, oh yes, I am also looking for some new pieces."

"Would you want to try the song you just played? I could accompany you on the piano."

"Of course," I said.

To my great surprise we did an unrehearsed number. The small crowd of admirers that surrounded him a little while before broke into thunderous applause asking for an encore. So we then played *Hating Gabi* another popular love song. Once more, I explained that I was there to look for new pieces that could be accompanied on the piano or guitar.

At Ping's suggestion I chose a semi-classical piece, *Pizzicato*, and another popular love song. For an encore we played some of the old numbers I knew almost by heart, *Kitten on the Keys,* and the *Blue Danube Waltz,* arrangement for marimba by Silos. I was immediately comfortable with his accompanying style so I asked him if he could possibly accompany me for the show at the UP. I asked him how much he would charge for doing the job, and he gallantly answered that it was he who should pay the fee for such a rare privilege

That was the beginning of our close association. A good show must be rehearsed well, so almost every afternoon when I did not have any pressing thing to do, I went to the Lyric Music House for rehearsals. And we always drew a small crowd of listeners each time. A distant relative who happened to be a constant attendant to those rehearsals vowed that if she would have a daughter when she got married she would make her learn to play the marimba. As it turned out, she fulfilled that promise. Her daughter Ernestina Crisologo became one of the best marimba players in the country.

The saying goes that familiarity breeds contempt. For Ping and myself, this was not so. The familiarity that those rehearsals generated was, surprisingly, a great fondness between the two of us.

Perhaps because of the novelty, we had to do several encores. Ping had a really good time and after that, he came to the UP whenever he had some free time from his work. He went first to the library where I was hurriedly preparing my lessons for the next day and then we would walk to the DHMH offices of Professor Romulo for my translating job. Once I was done, we would go and sit on the rocks that bordered the sea at the Roxas Boulevard and watch the glorious sunset.

Without spelling it out in so many words, we knew we were falling in love. For me it was a very different feeling from the way I felt for Roming some years before. First of all, I felt more mature. I was 21 years old and in a few more days I was finishing college and fulfilling the promise I had given to my father.

During that time, I hardly met with my gang because all of us were busy cleaning up our records and academic obligations in preparation for graduation. But they did notice that I no longer waited for them in the library as I did before, and neither did I ask them to walk me to the DMHM offices. They already saw who was walking with me. They had also noticed that I had lost my interest in swimming. At first the gang thought it was because Gening had graduated a semester before us and was no longer at the swimming area. But after they saw me going everywhere with Ping, they knew it was something different.

Meneling, much concerned, asked me point blank how I felt for Ping and I told him the truth as always. I told him I was in love with him but had no definite plans yet for the immediate future. I was still sort of leaving everything to fate at that point. .

"Just don't do anything foolish," he cautioned again. "And if he tries to be fresh and asks you to do something you shouldn't, let me know. I have not won my medal in Cornell for nothing." Meneling had won a gold medal in boxing at Cornell University in Ithaca N.Y. where he finished engineering cum laude.

"Don't worry about that. I wouldn't be that foolish," I assured him. "Besides, he has always been very refined and gentle."

My parents got to learn of my "new craze" and my father advised me to take my time. I was still young. I was bright and could go for further studies...perhaps in the US.

I told him I was not thinking of marriage yet. I planned to work after graduation and take my time enjoying my new life. But I definitely turned down his offer of going abroad for graduate studies.

My great excitement over my coming graduation was all mixed up. There was the feeling of triumph as well as relief because I was finishing something that I started after four years. At the same time, I was crazy in love with a handsome and talented man who was so tender...so tender and gentle in manner. What doubled my admiration for him was that he spoke Spanish beautifully thanks to his mother who taught Spanish before she got married. Gentle words uttered in Spanish, for me, had always taken on deeper meanings.

It was one of those evenings we spent on the big rugged rocks that guarded Roxas Boulevard from the Manila Bay. We watched the glowing sun slowly going down in all its final brilliance in the western horizon. Ping and I sat on the rocks holding hands and saying silly things. He called me Babe, his pet name for me. I suppose that was how he thought of me, someone young, someone to protect. As darkness slowly enveloped us, and the flickering streetlights took over the job of illumination, I felt his hand go around my waist, drawing me against him. Then, his mouth pressed onto mine in an impassioned kiss. Strangely, I did not resist it. I felt an urgent electrifying sensation that was beyond anything I had known before. Throughout it all, Ping was very tender and refined. He said he just wanted to let me know how much he really loved and wanted me.

That night I could not sleep well. I felt a sense of guilt for making a commitment when I had not even finished college. And yet, I also had a funny, strange desire that there should be more such expressions of love coming up.

The pile of work that was to be done for my coming graduation kept me from seeing him more than twice after that. Ping, too, was involved in the preparation for a jazz band that he was to take to Hongkong and Japan and other cities in Southeast Asia.

My parents and relatives, with the exception of Meneling, were all against him. They felt I could not be happy with one who had started but never finished college. They told me he was drunk with pride in being the King of Jazz and that he was a womanizer. Surely he would only make my life miserable. But I felt they did not know him as I did, never talked with him as we did, and with the memory of his gentleness, it was easy to turn a deaf ear to all their warnings. It was Meneling who took on the role of older brother. "You are old enough to know what is right and wrong and what will make you happy. Just don't get blinded by strong emotions. I believe you're still too young to sort all of these out. But, I am asking you not to do anything improper, if you know what I mean."

"Of course," I said." Don't worry."

About two weeks before graduation my head was really in a spin. There were still so many things I had to attend to. As soon as we got our blue slip indicating those who would graduate, I decided to focus all my thoughts on graduation and keep all the other troubling emotions on hold.

On the blue slip were so many things to do: sign for cap and gown, making sure one had the right color tassel, making sure of how our name should be written on the diploma, meet with the graduation chairman for instructions, and countless other details. I had already reserved the cap and gown and I knew the color of the Liberal Arts tassel. The name on my diploma should be my baptismal name, Baltasara, according to instructions from my father, and not the shortened Sarah. The rest of the blue slip instructions were easy to follow.

But I had to have my graduation dress since it would be the one I was to wear at the graduation party my father was giving after the program. I also had to get the invitations for my parents, *Tío* Ignacio and Poying who were glad to see me finish my college studies. I did not have to get one for Meneling because he was a member of the faculty of the Engineering Department and had to attend the ceremonies in cap and gown.

I found it a stroke of Fate that Ping was away from the country, for he would have surely insisted on attending the commencement ceremonies even at the risk of being snubbed by my family.

My sister had told me that the usual topic of conversation between my parents was my mother's great opposition to my relationship with Ping. Nene said that my father was not too worried about his not having finished college as long as he behaved like a gentleman with me. *Papá* was sure that, coming from very well-educated parents, Ping could not turn out to be a scoundrel. "I would rather have him loving my daughter than a lawyer or a senator or a wealthy husband who would treat his wife like a slave," my father would say, after which, according to my sister, *Mamá* would remain silent. But that matter did not bother me too much. I missed Ping, but I also was willing to leave Fate to take it from there.

After the graduation ceremonies were over, my father invited my gang and some professors and of course, my relatives to a dinner at Tom's Dixie Kitchen Night Club, a popular place for the elite in those times. Tom, the owner, an African-American who was an amiable fellow and well-liked by everyone had reserved the whole dining and dancing area for the occasion and decorated it elegantly with flowers and garlands. He also had a whole orchestra in full attendance. My heart was happy, but quite full of sadness realizing that all our four years of companionship had come to an end.

My father, sensing my innermost feelings tried to console me saying: "That is life, *hija*, it comes in stages, and you have to learn to take it. Otherwise it would be monotonous and you would get tired of it."

How true!

We went to our usual summer in Baguio but stayed there for only two weeks. I did not enjoy being there because my old friends were not there. We had already gone our separate ways. I insisted on going back home to Santa Cruz, but my mother said we had to go to Antipolo to give thanks to the Blessed Mother for my graduation from college. So there we stayed another two weeks.

All the time I was in Antipolo, I had already started to write letters, applying for jobs like secretary or assistant to lawyers or executives or teachers in different schools. My father said however that I did not have to look for a job right after my graduation. He had hoped I would go for graduate studies, perhaps in the United States.

I told him I did not want to waste time doing nothing. If I should choose to continue studying I could do it while I worked so I could pay my way. *Papá* said he could still afford to have me study, even send me abroad. But I told him that at my age I should already be acting like an adult. I asked him to give me that chance. He was sad but said nothing.

So I stayed in Santa Cruz preparing to find a job in Manila the coming June, for I knew I could not find anything challenging enough for me in that town. Then one fine day when I was losing all hope of ever getting a job because none of my letters were answered, my father called from his office.

"I was talking to Ding Fabella." he said. "He and his brother own the José Rizal College on R. Hidalgo Street in Manila and they need teachers for the coming school year. Are you interested?"

"Of course, I am," I answered excitedly. "At least I can start getting experience." And I called my old friend Juaning Falcon right away.

"I will teach at the José Rizal High School in Manila," I announced.

"Good," she said." At least we can see each other more often than when you were in the UP. Even Basiling can be with us, just like old times, no?"

Her brother Basiling was finishing a course in commerce at the Santo Tomas University, and he should have finished two years before but he got sick and had to stop.

During the summer Juaning came only three times to my home and we had a great time eating green mangoes with *bagoong* — salty tiny shrimps—and guavas from *Mamá*'s back garden. I did not mention to her that I had just found my great love. I did not want to talk about boyfriends because of the ugly town gossip that her brother was being groomed to be my future husband, something she surely did not know about. On the other hand she had not mentioned anything about her male friends either, though I heard there was a young doctor who was crazy about her.

That was the last time I saw Juaning.

I started teaching as soon as schools opened in June. My problem was where to live. My residence when I graduated was in Padre Faura, too far from my place of work so I would have to take the streetcar or have someone drive me to and from work. Once again *Papá* came to my rescue. He asked *Doña* Librada Avelino, still the D*irectora* of the *Centro Escolar de Señoritas* to allow me to board there. The place was within walking distance from my place of work. She kindly agreed.

It worked well for several months. I had a room in one of the houses where some of the faculty had their quarters for which I paid with my own money. I ate with the faculty. I was not restricted in my comings and goings, and if I had to be out until late at night I simply had to leave word with the one who had the key to the Infirmary, the place where the sick students were, and let her know when I was coming home.

The school also needed a teacher in Social Sciences so I recommended my close friend, Nitang Molina, and she was readily hired. I could not have asked for a better arrangement.

On weekends, Meneling or Poying or my father would pick me up and we would have lunch at some fancy restaurant and perhaps take in a movie after that, or do some shopping. On Sundays, I heard Mass at the church of my childhood, the San Sebastian Church and from there go to the beauty salon right in front of the *Centro* where Mr. Avelino, the brother of *Doña* Librada would cut or set my hair in preparation for the coming week.

All that time, Ping was abroad with his band. He wrote me almost every week, sweet little notes of love, not as florid or poetic like Roming's but full of adult wisdom...about life and love. He said he missed me very much but playing abroad was one way he could earn money and save for a dream family of the future. I answered him in letters full of endearment. He always addressed his letters to the school because at the *Centro*, letters to me would be put together with hundreds of others for the students and faculty and I would not get it right away.

Once again, I had the feeling that I was on the brink of something, something that was about to happen. I had started on a teaching career, I was deeply in love with one who said he loved me...but I wasn't quite sure what would happen next.

## *Chapter Seven*

Ping called me as soon as was back in Manila and asked if he could pick me up after my class. I told him I would be upset if he didn't. I was just as eager to see him.

We had a light dinner and then we drove around before going to the Luneta right up to the big boulders that bordered Manila Bay. This time, we didn't sit on the rocks. We just stopped and sat in the park where it was dark to enjoy the cool breeze and the full moon. We kissed and he told me how much he had missed me during the time he was gone. He said there were women who always followed a band, something that could never be helped, but they were not the kind that he enjoyed being with.

Then he changed the subject and told me that he knew my parents and relatives did not look on him favorably for many reasons among which was the fact that he did not have any college degree. Manila's elite was small, he said, and gossip went around fast. He explained why he had turned to jazz from the classical piano he had started with. He told me how much he loved jazz and how creative he thought it was. It was not learning a musical piece exactly as someone else had written it, but it was improvising, bringing in one's interpretation to music that someone else wrote. Jazz gave one's creativity a chance to find expression both in tone as well as rhythm. I had never seen him talk about anything so animated. Besides, he said, in closing the topic, he earned money with it.

I told him that *Papá* was hoping I would go for graduate studies abroad and I assured him that I did not care to do so. I wanted to be independent for a while, earning my own way and making my own decisions. He said he was glad I felt that way. We talked a lot about serious matters—what we wanted from life, what we thought about the future—then we would break off and tease, and laugh, just happy being there together. When we ran out of things to say and the silence took over, he brought me home.

It took me a while to get to sleep. I kept tossing and turning in bed, going over the things we said, analyzing my feelings, not only of sheer happiness but also of a certain unqualified longing which I could not define, knowing only that I wanted something more from him. I wondered whether that was all there ever would be between us—the joy of being together, the hugging and kissing—then the parting. I was not unaware of his reputation, and yet, I believed I saw a side of the man that was the Ping he truly was. And it was that man I had fallen in love with.

The next day I was almost late for my first class but I managed to get through it and from there went to the salon. Why is it that a trip to the beauty parlor always lightens a woman's spirits. As I walked in, Mr. Avelino, who had been doing my hair for so long, asked me if I was sick. According to him I looked wilted. So I told him that was the reason I had come...so he could do something with my hair that would make me feel and look better.

Perhaps what I really wanted was for Ping to be around more often and give me assurances of how much I meant to him. Or it might have been the special warmth he radiated...the way I felt...when he held me very close to his heart which I had never felt from others, including my father. I prayed for assistance to the Blessed Mother every night. The big question that continued to bug me though was, after such passionate kisses, then what?

At the *Centro* I had no personal telephone that I could use to call him any time I wanted to. I had to use the school phone to talk to him very briefly telling him when and where we could meet. I would have loved to go out with him every day but that was impossible because he was in the midst of negotiations for his band's contract to play at two clubs, the Army and Navy Club and the Manila Polo Club. So I had to be satisfied for the two or three meetings we could have together during the week. It was just too difficult to synchronize our working schedules. When I was working during the day he was resting from his job of going from playing in two clubs at night. To be with me he had to rush over or report late for his evening gigs giving some lame excuse. I had to be content with that. Beggars just could not be choosers and I was begging for more time with him.

My parents came on alternate weekends to take me to lunch or to go shopping for clothes or other unimportant things that I actually did not need. We usually ate at some big restaurant owned by one of my mother's customers who bought vegetables and other things from the farm every week. *Mamá* always told me that if I needed any money I could go to any of them and ask for some. She also opened a credit account in several stores at the Escolta, but I never allowed her to pay for my debts.

One weekend in September she came with the news that there would be a big wedding in Santa Cruz. Carmen Ongkiko, from one of the town's wealthy families, was marrying a doctor and the family had asked my mother to let me be the maid of honor.

"Why?" I asked quite disgusted at the idea. "Usually the maid of honor is the bride's best friend, or at least, a close relative. I hardly know her except for meeting her occasionally at parties and picnics."

"Oh, perhaps she knows that we can afford to pay for the lovely dress that will complement the bride's gown. It will be made by a big name fashion designer." *Mamá* tried to impress me.

"I am neither impressed nor thrilled," I remarked. "Besides, I believe I am already too old for such things."

"And do you know who the best man is?" *Mamá* continued, not paying any attention to my remarks.

"I couldn't care less," I said. She didn't realize that telling me would annoy me even more. Somehow I had already sensed what was coming.

"It's your former playmate Basiling. Aren't you glad?"

"His sister was my playmate...when we were small...not anymore." I had already started to see red, remembering the rumors that had been going around.

*Mamá* was openly surprised at my sour remark, but I could not help it. Being reminded of the cruel gossip spread around by her friends, that Basiling was being groomed to be my husband, I had raised my voice and spoken rudely. Poor boy, he probably had no idea of what was going on. Realizing this, I told my mother I was sorry, but I didn't really want to be a maid of honor, not for someone whom I did not consider a closer friend. I also did not like the obvious "show and tell" affair that the wedding was turning out to be. My father often said "cross your bridges when you come to them," so I dismissed the news as something to be dealt with later.

**M**y relationship with Ping was keeping me preoccupied. There was no question in my mind that I loved him and he was the only man I could ever fall in love with. Even just thinking about him would get me excited beyond measure—the way he was gentle with me, the way we saw eye to eye on so many things, and when he held me close to him it just felt that nothing in the world could harm me. But after each time he took me home and I got into bed, the nagging doubts would come. "And then what? Is this all there is to it?" I believed that most sweethearts, aware of where the relationship was taking them would begin to talk about definite plans for the future. But aside from the burning kisses that thrilled me to the core of my being when we were together, the subject never came up in our conversations.

So at one of our sunset meetings, I very tactfully said I wondered how long these meetings would last. Perhaps Ping already sensed that somehow the question would come up soon because he was ready with an answer. He straightened up, held my hand, kissed it and said:

"Babe, don't ever t think that I'm using these happy moments we're together as enjoyable trysts to pass my time. We may be the same age, but I'm much older than you as far as life matters are concerned. I don't want you to think that the way I feel for you is just a wild spark of infatuation that will eventually fade and leave you only with deep regret. That's no way to live. It would be a miserable existence. I can honestly tell you that every moment with you is something I look forward to. I will admit that I have known women here and abroad before I met you, but momentary pleasure is how I would describe my time with them. No feelings remained in my heart, nor do I have any true affection or regard for any of them. With you, my feelings are absolutely different. The way I feel for you is real, and deep and, I hope, lasting. You have to trust me on that.

He had noticed my reaction when he mentioned he had known other women, but he immediately sought to relieve it by holding me close and kissing me. After he said all that, my young mind, dulled by my almost insane love for him was easily appeased. I did trust him.

"For me, you are a sacred icon," he continued. "I must not rush you. I want you to know me well—listen to all the things people say about me—especially those coming from your parents and relatives. I want you to see me bare, the way I truly am, without anything hidden—physically and emotionally—so you can be certain that it is the real me who loves you and whom you love."

For the first time, I was calm about our relationship and assured that he loved me as much as I loved him. I reasoned that I was in no hurry to get married and have children. My mother had told me a million times that I should go slowly. "Go to parties, get to know other men.

You may find someone that you can love more than you love him." But I could not be swayed. Ping and I continued to see each other whenever his schedule and mine would allow it and he lost no opportunity to tell me and show me how much he loved me.

Sometime in October on a day Ping and I were to meet, my mother suddenly came to Manila to take me to the dressmaker who was going to make my gown for the wedding in November at which I was to be the maid of honor. I realized I had not yet told Ping about the wedding, so I lost no time in letting him know, telling him that I really did not want to be a part of it because my parents' friends were pairing me off with Basiling, who would be the best man. I felt him immediately bristle at the very thought of it.

"Why did you accept?" he asked, his voice shaking. "Why didn't you tell your mother you don't like the idea at all?" The vehemence of his reaction surprised me.

"I did but she wouldn't listen to me. Besides, no matter what anyone says or does, nobody can force me to marry anyone I do not love."

"I only pray that you stick by that," Ping said.

"You can rely on me, sweetheart," I assured him as I kissed him.

And I meant it. After that, we swore eternal love and told each other that nothing would ever change how we felt for one another.

The next time we met after that, he held me close and said, "I want to take you as my God-given bride. However much I am sorely tempted to ravish you here and now in answer to my need, I shall control myself, for I do not want to desecrate a sacred icon. So let us just be happy with loving kisses and warm hugs...for now." I wholly agreed. But as the month of November came, he was more and more against my being a maid of honor at the coming wedding. Then one day, about the second week of that month he suddenly said to me: "Babe, sweetheart, why don't we get married before that wedding takes place, huh? Wouldn't that be great? Wouldn't you like that?"

"O my God!" I gasped. " You must be kidding! My parents would kill me."

" I would rather see you dead than in the arms of another man."

"Oh, c'mon, Ping. Don't you trust me? I assure you nothing can come out of it."

He kept quiet and I thought that was the end of it. What I did not realize was that he was actually seething.

Two weeks after that when we were having lunch in a small restaurant in Plaza Goiti, he took hold of my two hands, looked at me seriously and said:

"Now I want to test how much you love me. I've made up my mind that we're getting married on the Friday before that wedding."

"WHAT?" I almost choked. I couldn't think of what to say, so I remained quiet. Ping kept holding my hand and looking at me. His eyes were serious, but he was smiling and I could never resist look. So I told him it was my turn to talk. "If you want it that badly, why not now?" I teased.

Ping did not answer right away. He must have sensed I was teasing, but it seems he had already thought everything out. "Because I do not want to inconvenience too many people. I have to prepare all the details needed. If we elope just before the weekend, there will be less trouble in your school because they can find a substitute. Your parents would normally be picking you up so it would not be too obvious."

I could not say anything. It would mean we would have only six days to do everything. I thought of all the papers I had to correct, my laundry to pick up that Saturday, and so many other little details that one carries out on a daily basis. But it was the only way I could be with the man I truly loved for the rest of my life.

Then I thought of what my elopement would do to my parents. After all, they were not really the ones pairing me off to Basiling. It was their friends and the town gossips who could not mind their own business. But it was *Papá* and *Mamá* who would suffer most from what I was about to do.

When the day came, I packed two changes of clothing in a small bag and put it aside, ready to pick up any time. I paid the laundry woman for the clothes she had cleaned and told her I had no dirty ones for I was going on vacation. I arranged my clothes and books in three boxes and left only what I would wear that Friday.

There was a confused mixture of happiness, sadness and guilt. How would my parents take my sudden disappearance?

But knowing how much Ping loved me, I could not ignore his ultimatum. Besides, I really wanted to be with him. He was always so gentle, so attentive. It showed in the way he treated me, the way he looked at me, and in his warm caresses. I prayed to God to bless my decision since it was He who allowed me to get this far with my love.

The only one who knew about our plans was Nitang Molina, my bosom friend. I think she was even more nervous than I was.

The night before I eloped I prayed the Rosary before the image of the Blessed Mother, fervently asking her for forgiveness for what I was about to do.

On the day I was supposed to go with Ping I felt all strung up like a wired toy. I left my bag of clothing with Mr. Avelino across the street and told him I would pick it up after my class. I cleaned my room very well and even left my keys on the dresser near the nightstand. My heart was heavy but the promise of heavenly joy with Ping gave me all the energy I needed. I was very good to my pupils in school that day and I told them to be good and prepare their lessons every day.

After classes I found Ping and Nitang waiting for me. They asked me if I wanted to eat anything and I said I did not have any appetite at all.

There was a big swanky car that I had never seen Ping driving before.

"That is our *Ninong's*\* car," Ping said.

"And where are we going?' I asked feeling suddenly short of breath.

"We're going to my aunt's place in San Pedro Makati. She's getting the Justice of the Peace to perform the ceremony."

The aunt Ping referred to was *Tía* Nena, the widow of *Tío* Eduardo Jimenez, and owner of what at that time was the biggest house in the town of San Pedro Makati, fondly called Sampiro by the townspeople. Facing the Pasig River, it had a big living room, four bedrooms and a spacious dining room adjoining a kitchen. Ping was very close to this aunt who took care of him when he was very young. It was she who approved of the elopement and even promised to get the Justice of the Peace of the town to go to her house for the marriage ceremony.

I was seated beside Ping as he drove the car to *Tía* Nena's house. He took my hand and noticed it was very cold. I was very quiet

"You nervous, Babe, sweetheart? You're not going to change your mind about this are you?"

"Oh no! I was just thinking of my father. How hurt and ashamed he must be feeling."

When we arrived at *Tía* Nena's house we were informed that the Justice of the Peace was in another town and would not be available until the next day.

I was terribly disappointed. But *Tía* Nena had prepared some delicious dishes that served as *"merienda-cena."*\*\* for the group. Perico Limjap, married to former beauty queen, Neny Apacible, was our sponsor and he said he was available the following afternoon so *Tía* Nena said everything was working out just fine,

Because we were not yet legally married, *Tía* Nena, a real stickler for correct conduct, did not allow us to sleep in one room. She gave me her daughter Leticia's bed and Ping slept in Totong's room. Needless

---

\**sponsor, traditionally for baptisms and weddings*
\*\**High tea*

to say I hardly slept at all. It was a strange house and the reason I was there was even stranger. In the morning, Letty was very nice and helpful to me. She gave me a towel and showed me the bathroom so I could wash up and look clean and fresh for this special day.

We were married that afternoon on the 25th of November almost at the same time as the big wedding in Santa Cruz where I was supposed to have been the maid of honor.

After a lavish dinner cooked by *Tía* Nena's brother, *Tío* Inong and his wife *Tía* Etang, we retired to Leticia's bedroom. Letty was to sleep in her mother's room.

By then Ping and I were both very hungry for each other, but even before Ping proceeded to undress me, he first talked to me briefly.

"Babe, sweetheart," he began, "What we are about to do is the crowning glory of our relationship. You know I love you very much and I would not want to hurt you for anything in the world. But you are a virgin and it is going to hurt you at first. I will try to be as gentle as possible and we'll do something about the pain later." Indeed it hurt very much but his words of love and his caresses made me forget the pain.

In the morning *Tía* Nena came to change the bed linen. She wanted to see if I had stained and she hugged me with tears in her eyes when she saw that I had. She said, "Thank you, *hija*, for being a virgin for Ping." I didn't make any sense of why she came up with that. Wasn't that usually the case? Only much later did I get to know the significance of her remark at the time.

Once Ping and I had calmed down, I started to get very worried over how my parents had taken the disappointment and shame I knew they were feeling over my elopement. So I called Meneling. The moment he heard my voice he asked: "Where are you? Are you now married? Can I come and see you?"

I assured him I was fine and told him that I was married the day before. I gave him *Tía* Nena's address so he could come to see me. He told me not to call anybody else because they were all still very angry, thinking I had been forced to do what I had done.

Early the next morning he was at *Tía* Nena's doorstep. I was so happy to see him and Julita, his wife, who had stood by me all this time. He was all smiles as he kissed me on my forehead as he always did and asked: "So, how does it feel being married, my dear?"

"Oh, Ling, It was very painful at his first attempt," I burst out and I buried my face in his chest.

"I know, Baby, but that is the initiation rite all women must go through as their welcome to the sorority of wives. Now remember, it is your duty never to refuse him that pleasure."

And I kept that in mind always.

But it seemed to me that all the pent-up desire suppressed into frustration that Ping and I both felt before our marriage had to be given vent. After the initial discomfort that was alleviated by simple medication, making love became a delightful experience. Remembering Meneling's words, I was always ready for Ping. Any place where we were left alone for more than an hour was an opportunity for our union to find expression. Once we were invited to a picnic held at his uncle's farm. There, the air was cool and the sun was bright and under the trunk of a huge spreading mango tree, we found ecstatic joy. These habitual pleasures continued for several months until I started to feel uneasy with the obvious signs of pregnancy

Our church wedding took place a week after our civil ceremony in the hundred-year-old Catholic church of the town, quite near the house. The sponsors were Perico Limjap and *Tía* Nena, my maid of honor was Nitang Molina. Ping's best man was his cousin, Alfredo. Of my relatives, only Meneling was present.

There was a little feast after the ceremony prepared by *Tío* Inong aided by many other relatives who lived in San Pedro Makati—*Tía* Tansing,

*Tío* Enchong, *Tío* Siano and *Tía* Yvonne. I was lucky for my in-laws were very good to me. Unfortunately, Ping's parents could not be there because his father, a practicing lawyer, was away from Manila and his mother was indisposed.

After our wedding many of my father's friends who knew me as a child and had seen how close I was to my father, offered to accompany us to go to my parents to make peace in case we were afraid to do so ourselves. One of them was Senator Claro M. Recto, at the time already a fierce defender of national pride and against all types of exploitation from foreigners. He used to live in Santo Sepulcro St, near *Tío* Badong's house and remembered the way I used to read his poems. Loleng, a cousin, and I used to play with his first wife, Angelita, when we went out to their garden. The Senator called me and told me he would go with us to Santa Cruz if we were afraid to be rebuffed by my parents. Another friend was Judge Guillermo Guevara who happened to be living with my parents when I was born. I thanked all of them for their concern but I also told them I did not think we would need an escort. *Papá* had always told me to face the truth and do things the right way, and Ping and I had already decided we would go there by ourselves. If they refused to see us or decided to insult us by sending us away, then we would come home.

Meneling told me that he had spoken to my father and told him we were properly married in church and that I was very happy with Ping. He told me that *Papá* admitted that my decision to elope was partly their fault for being so much against my relationship with Ping and being so negative about him. When they heard that I was pregnant, my mother got very excited saying she hoped it would be a boy.

I myself was praying to St. Anthony to help me ask God for a boy.

So one fine Friday morning, Ping and I motored to Santa Cruz to ask for my parents' blessings. There were the expected tears of both regret and joy. My mother had her cook prepare a sumptuous meal for us and she telephoned the farm to send some vegetables and fruit, plenty of corn and two sacks of rice for us to take back to Manila.

*Mamá* asked me about my pregnancy and I told her it was quite normal. I had a few weeks of slight nausea but then everything was all right after that. I told her that my obstetrician was Dr. Jose Genato Sr., head of the Ob/Gyn Department of Santo Tomas Hospital. She disapproved of a male doctor for obstetrics and she strongly recommended Dr. Potenciana Kabigting, a relative, who was with the Philippine General Hospital. She wanted to entrust me to her care and assured me she would do a good job of taking care of me during my pregnancy.

From the attic of the house she had her maid bring out an old but well-preserved basket, which she had used for my baby clothes. She wanted me to use them for my coming child. In it was an odd list of what one should have for a newly born infant. And then she gave me a wallet with a hefty three hundred pesos in it, a pretty big sum in those days. We stayed for two days and came home Sunday because Ping had to attend to his two bands.

When we got home I was surprised that I did not feel tired at all after the two-hour ride from Santa Cruz. Ping suggested a shower and we went straight to the bathroom. Once again, I wondered where my husband got all his energy. We never even made it to the bed. When I reminded him to be careful with my pregnancy he simply smiled and said, "Sweetheart, babies are like flowers; they need to be nurtured."

Ping was crazy over the prospect of being a father and one day he had a book from which he was choosing a name for the baby.

"That's too late," I said. "I already promised St. Anthony I would name our boy after him." So he threw the book away and kissed my tummy and from then on, always referred to the baby as Tony as if he knew it was a boy and already in the world.

After more than two months of living with *Tía* Nena we moved to a small *entresuelo**. It had a spacious bedroom, a living-dining room, a kitchen and a clean, well-equipped bathroom. It was also quite near to where Ping's parents lived. There was, however, one problem. While Ping had to attend to his bands at night, I would be alone in the apartment. My mother-in-law came to our rescue by assigning Nick, whom the family called Onching, to live with me. My mother then hired a maid who could do the cleaning and the laundry and preparation of breakfast. Onching would go to school early in the morning and come home in the afternoon before Ping left at seven.

After supper, each of us would do our own thing. Onching spent the time preparing his lessons, reading and writing until late at night and I did some crochet or helped the maid to tidy up in the kitchen. Domesticity had come to my life.

My mother's next visit saw her bringing some fancy equipment for the kitchen.

"These are the latest modern, energy-saving equipment," she said. "I got them for you and I think you should learn how to use them."

There was a full-size electric range that came with a big book of recipes. *Mamá* knew me well. I only knew how to fry an egg and cook some bacon or sausage for breakfast.

Then she also brought me a brand new sewing machine. I did not know how to sew but I had learned how to crochet, knit, tat and embroider. *Mamá* suggested that I study in what was then a popular school called Kollermann School of Fashion or the Petit Paris, but I decided that sewing would come after I had the baby. It was more important for me to learn how to cook first.

I enrolled in a home school run by a lady, Mrs. Lusonghap, who taught mostly Chinese dishes. After only three sessions I stopped because I did not think Ping and I needed such fancy dishes every day. Following a friend's advice I went to Mrs, Cuyugan's classes and

*<sub></sub>*a one-floor apartment with a mezzanine*

learned many choice Filipino and Spanish dishes. What I really wanted to know though was how to do ordinary Filipino dishes like *sinigang na baboy o isda*, or *tortang giniling*, or *inihaw na baboy*, etc.

A relative, Fe Ladameo, who was teaching Home Economics at a local school, gave me some step-by-step instructions on how to cook two or three of Ping's favorite recipes. Other dishes, I learned from my favorite fish vendor in the market. Onching and I went to the Paco market for fish. This vendor, who cleaned them for an additional fee of five centavos, gave us step-by-step instructions on how to cook some every day dishes, nothing fancy nor expensive, but very good. Whenever my parents came to Manila to visit and inquire about their coming grandson they were surprised at how fast I had learned how to cook and how quickly I was improving as a housewife.

Mamá also bought us a set of dining-room furniture for six, very simple but sturdy, keeping in mind that it would have to withstand abuse from future children. Titang, Meneling's wife, gave me a whole set of party dishes, in case we decided to hold parties and my mother-in-law and her sister, *Tía* Naty, took care of the matching tablecloth and napkins. Not to be left behind, Poying's gift was the necessary set of flatware—simple and well-designed. All these encouraged me to take housewifely duties very seriously.

Having learned how to cook, I then squeezed in some time to learn how to sew. I knew that once the children came they would need clothes. *Papá* took care of my tuition fees for sewing school. I loved my sewing lessons because it opened up a world of artistic ideas in which I could use my knowledge of painting. As my pregnancy progressed normally, I turned my attention to decorating our bedroom and designating a little space for the nursery.

In those times, some seventy years ago, twin beds were the prevailing style for married couples instead of the big matrimonial bed. This is perhaps the more practical way of thinking since usually, only half of the double bed is actually used as the occupants invariably lie very close together preferring to share each other's warmth or satisfying each other's desires. As I write this now, I recall the many times I had to answer my children and grandchildren's questions as to why there was such a classification of "twin" with respect to beds and related articles when there was only one bed to be considered. Over and over I had to tell them that once upon a time their grandparents had to sleep in separate beds for health reasons, and, I was quite tempted to add, perhaps to regulate pregnancies as well.

We had two beautifully designed beds—my father's gift—as soon as we moved to this tiny apartment. My first sewing lessons found me making simple bedspreads complete with matching curtains and a little cover for the nightstand that separated the two beds. Ping was very happy over my accomplishments as a housewife. He also marveled at my increasing expertise in cooking. I thought this quite a compliment considering that his mother was an excellent cook. He also never failed to reward me in his own way of providing glorious ecstatic pleasure and it never mattered on whose bed it happened although most of the time only one bed was used throughout the night.

Ping said perhaps the expected baby was bringing us good luck financially. He remarked that there was a company of vaudeville players—a very enjoyable intermission offering of musical numbers between films—and he had been approached for a band to accompany the numbers. He would still have the two bands in the two nightclubs with this program in the afternoons and evenings. So things started to look up. I was delighted with that piece of news and admired his efforts to earn more. I thought that perhaps we could quickly start saving for a small house.

*I* really enjoyed everything I was doing in this new phase of my life. Onching provided the communicative exchange that I needed while

Ping was busy with his jobs. My young brother-in-law was always full of stories about the lives of saints, as if these were part of his lessons. So one day, I asked him, "Where do you get all this stuff?"

"Well, after class I walk to Intramuros and sit in one of the libraries of the several religious orders there, and I read and read a lot of very interesting stories about what happened a long time ago."

"What?" I asked, surprised. "You walk from your school to Intramuros?"

"Yes," he said nonchalantly, "it isn't really that far."

"What time is school over?"

"One-thirty. Then we have games and I don't like to play games. So I just walk to one of the big church libraries there."

"*Naku*! That's why your shoes never last long. But, at least, you get good physical and mental exercise!" I remarked.

I realized much later in life that it must have been in that period that Onching was starting to store the vast wealth of knowledge of history and beautiful language that was to form the basis of the celebrated writings of National Artist, Nick Joaquin.

## Chapter Eight

Acting upon the doctor's advice, I started doing exercises for advancing pregnancy. I continued to beseech the favors of St. Anthony of Padua and attended Mass every Tuesday, a day especially dedicated to St. Anthony, and my novena prayers asking for a boy continued. Everyone knew that novenas to St. Anthony for that purpose usually succeeded. Onching often accompanied me while he was on vacation but since school had already started the maid came with me instead. Sometimes Ping would come but I never woke him up to do so since he usually came home late. After church I would usually go to the market to get the things we would need for the meals of the week. And once back home, there always seemed to be a million things to do.

There was the cooking for the day's meal, the sewing of draperies and the preparation of the things necessary for the baby's coming. I was glad for these many things that occupied my mind and hands.

Then all of a sudden it was already June and my body had changed into that of a big-bellied expectant mother, happily awaiting my initiation to motherhood. All this time, Ping gave me his loving support and I was appreciative of that.

According to my doctor's calculations, he said the baby was due about the first week of September, but because I was physically on the go and emotionally prepared, the birth might even come earlier. I never really worried or gave it a thought and left it to the Blessed Mother to help me when the time came for that blessed event.

One Friday evening, just as we were going into the last week of August, Ping suggested that we have a light supper and catch the last screening of a movie. "Pretty soon you'll be tied up with the baby you won't be able to go out for some time," he said. So we went to one of the downtown movie houses, but I can no longer recall what the picture was.

At about ten o'clock I felt a bit queasy and thought it might have been something I had eaten, so I paid no particular attention to it. But about ten minutes later I felt something burst inside me and in a split second I found myself wet all over. I realized it was a prelude to childbirth and Ping guided me nervously to the car to go to the hospital.

A cousin, *Ate* Elena Lagdameo, wife of then National Treasurer, Salvador Lagdameo, had been requested by my mother to accompany me and take over when the baby came. Ping called her as soon as we arrived at the Philippine General Hospital. In the meantime the doctor on duty was called.

"Oh, that will take another fifteen to eighteen more hours of labor," he said. You can still go home, take a shower and come for the final labor."

But when Ping called *Ate* Elena, she was frantic.

"Get a room and wait there." She was insistent. "I'll be there in twenty minutes."

When *Ate* Elena arrived I was already in labor. I was wheeled to the labor room where Dr. Kabigting was waiting for me. By midnight the pains came faster and sharper and Tony came into the world at 12:57 as August 24$^{th}$ was just starting. He came out with a loud wail but even before that, he did something rarely heard in the delivery room. He give out a loud "Achoo!" making Ping remark, "Now that baby is certainly my son!" for Ping too sneezes many times every morning. Everyone in the delivery room was genuinely surprised. How could a first delivery be so quick and easy? I was glad and thankful to the Blessed Mother for making my delivery relatively painless.

The first thing that Ping did after holding and admiring his son was to call his parents and then notify mine by long distance about the happy event. My parents came two days later, both of them dressed as if they were going to a big fiesta. When my mother saw Tony she picked him up despite the disapproval of the Nursery Room nurse. My father asked Ping if he had passed out the customary cigars and my husband had to admit he had forgotten to do so. Besides becoming a new father, he was also occupied with the vaudeville program, which his friend, Adolfo López, a Spanish director of stage plays had dropped on his lap.

"Well, it is not too late to do that," *Papá* said as he placed on the table, five boxes of Corona cigars to be distributed among the male doctors in the Obstetrics Department. I remember that one of the doctors said, "This is the first time I see the grandfather distributing cigars instead of the father."

With such an ordinary and quite uneventful first delivery, I did not have to stay in the hospital more than six days. My mother stayed with me while my father went back to Santa Cruz where he again proudly distributed cigars among his friends. Even the manager and some tenants in the farm got cigars which they kept like sacred souvenirs since they did not smoke at all.

It was *Mamá* who woke up in the middle of the night to bring the baby to me for feeding. She slept on Ping's bed while he used the big sofa in the living room. That was very convenient because the poor fellow had to go out after breakfast for the rehearsals and came home about ten at night. This way he did not bother anybody.

After three weeks of breastfeeding, I had no more milk. No amount of juices and soups or hand massage could coax my breasts to give enough milk to satisfy my son. So he started on bottlefeeding under the supervision of my doctor. Happily, there were no adverse results.

By that time, I was strong enough to continue what I was doing before the delivery. My mother then broached the subject of taking Tony with her to Santa Cruz. She said that I had too many plans and activities and she was afraid that I might neglect the baby. Deep in my heart I knew that she was longing to hold the boy close to her bosom. I had the same longings for my son but I was quite ready to give him to her for a while so to make up, in a very small way, for what hurt I gave them by my unexpected elopement.

I had to do a lot of explaining to Ping about this matter. He was reluctant, but he also reasoned out that since we were both busy—me with my newly acquired skills in cooking and sewing and he with his rehearsals with the new group, there was the possibility that Tony might be neglected at times. As soon as my mother found out that we had agreed to let her have the baby, she immediately hired a registered nurse to take care of him and went out to buy the necessary things needed for the best nursery she could think of for Baby Tony's use in Santa Cruz.

My heart ached to see my son leaving me even before we got used to each other but when I think of the great sorrow my elopement had caused my parents, my own sadness seemed petty. Ping also missed Tony but he agreed to it for the same reasons that I had. Both of us accepted the fact that Tony was better off with his grandparents, at least for the time being. Ping had accepted the job of providing the music for the new vaudeville company that was to play at the Savoy theatre. He was very busy with the music for the show. Ping had a very good friend in the person of Adolfo López, the Spanish stage director of *zarzuelas* and Spanish comedies. Adolfo was a fine Spanish stage director whose unusually creative talent in music and the arts gave him an uninterrupted income from novelty shows, school performances, national festivals and the movies. He was born of Spanish parents in Manila but for reasons unknown to me he had no living relatives in the country. I knew that at one time he had gone to visit some of them in Barcelona but he always came back to the land of his birth.

Since Ping and I got married, Adolfo had kept his distance but when the producers of the projected vaudeville program approached him and asked him to direct it he could think only of Ping to help him with it. Ping and I talked about the new job that was offered to him. I didn't know what to think, so said nothing to Ping. On the one hand, I was happy with the thought that we would have time to enjoy our baby and could then resume our love making which had been put on hold during the last two months of my pregnancy. But I also realized that as parents we had the responsibility to think about the future of our children, because I was sure there would be more. Ping's extra job would bring in more money and this would help us save for the proverbial rainy day. The extra job would mean that he would be working day and night and I might not have as much time with him as I wanted, but there were also many things I could do at home.

Those were truly very lonely days for me. Ping left at ten in the morning for rehearsals and came back about four or five in the afternoon. We would have some brief moments together, sometimes an occasional outburst of love, and then supper. Then Ping would leave for work as pianist for a stage or doing solo performances in several clubs like the Army Navy Club, Casino Español, and the Manila Polo Club. It was a grueling schedule but at least his Mondays were free.

I had to learn to adjust to that schedule but I kept myself busy with sewing. After Tony was born, I quickly lost all the pounds that I had gained when I was pregnant. I crocheted several things for the house, like kitchen towels, runners, pot holders and who knows what else, but the days went by. Then came the opening night of the vaudeville intermission. Ping insisted that I be there to meet the whole troupe, especially its three stars, Mary, Nena, Chiqui (not their real names), and I'm glad I went, for I had been feeling very lonely with Tony away and Ping gone most of the day

It was an entertaining show, fast paced and well directed. I was sure it would bring in more money to the Savoy Theatre. The stars were pretty and had foreign features: two had American fathers, and the third one was half Russian. They had tall, lithe and slim bodies that they showed off in their scanty costumes. Nena had a sweet, angelic face but it was Mary who caught everyone's attention. She had what one would call a statuesque Greek presence. There was a chorus line of about a dozen lassies from local talents who supplied excellent dancing and singing complements. For variety, there was a couple of Negro tap-dancers who rendered fancy jazz routines, and a stage "magician" who delighted the younger audience with his amazing tricks.

The performers were all very friendly as most show people tend to be. Even Adolfo López, the Spanish-Filipino director was quite charming with me, perhaps because I was the only one who communicated with him in Spanish.

Their regular show was to open several days before Thanksgiving and was scheduled to go on to the third week of December when the Christmas extravaganza would be shown through the 6$^{th}$ of January. This would mean even more rehearsals and I did my best to face the bitter reality that Ping would have very little time left for me. But I had no choice. So I tried to occupy myself with little things that would be useful for the family.

Ping usually came home after the second show at 5:30 and we would have dinner together before he would leave to play with the other bands. Often, he just went to the Polo Club where there was always a bigger crowd but would also call the Army and Navy Club to see if there was any problem. I told him that he really did not have to work that hard. He was burning the candle on both ends and I worried about what it would do to his health. Even our love making dwindled to a minimum, and try as we did, the impassioned enjoyment of mutual desires that we had before the baby came, was no longer there. I surmised that it was because he was too tired to be an ardent lover or we had suddenly grown old after only two years of marriage. But I never gave him any hint of my observations for I thought it would bother him and seem that I was not appreciative of what he was doing for the family,

Mercifully, my life was about to take another turn. It was one of those lonely days when I was cutting a blouse for myself that the telephone rang. I was wondering who it could be for my mother had just left with Tony for Santa Cruz after a week-end visit with me.

A man's voice greeted me. "Hello! Sarah Joaquin? This is Dr. Nicanor Reyes, your former Economics professor. Do you remember me?" He was a Doctor of Philosophy holder.

"Oh, yes, sir," I answered quite flustered by the unexpected call. "What can I do for you?"

"A little bird told me that your son is with your mother, is this true?"

"Well, yes sir. My mother wanted to enjoy him first because she never had a baby boy. But she brings him here frequently to visit."

Dr. Reyes stated quite formally, 'I'm going directly to the point." He then added, "I am contacting all my former bright students because I have started a school of Accounting and I would like to know if you would be interested in joining us." He said with much enthusiasm.

"Thank you, Dr. Reyes for the compliment, but I know nothing about Accounting at all. My major field is in the arts."

"I know but the approved curriculum includes English and Spanish and I am sure you can very well teach both."

"On that, certainly, sir. And I would love to join you. But I have to discuss this with my husband first."

"Of course. You let me know your decision in a week, can you?"

"Absolutely!"

I was literally on cloud nine and I put away my blouse for a while and opened my closet to see if I had enough clothes to wear that were presentable enough for teaching college students. I was sure that Ping would refuse at first. He had some notions about wives staying at home, but I knew how to convince him so he would agree. Besides, it would be another source of income for us.

When he came home that evening he looked exhausted and I was reluctant to even ask him whether he was sick. He gave me a perfunctory kiss and dropped into our one and only sofa and did not move for a long while.

"Are you feeling all right? Is anything wrong?" I asked.

"Not really. I just got a notice from the Army and Navy Club that they would close the night club in two weeks. I don't really blame them. I had neglected that band since we started rehearsing for the vaudeville show."

"Well, that isn't the end of the world," I said to soothe him and I started to give him a neck massage. Remember what *Papá* said? "*Quien mucho abarca, poco aprieta.*"* You were holding three jobs at the same time. I was afraid that if you kept much longer at it, all you would get was a nervous breakdown."

"Maybe, you're right. Anyway, what I earn at this new job is more than enough to make up for the loss of one."

"And I have a surprise for you! You'd never guess," I teased him.

He looked at me, wrinkled his brows and said, "You're pregnant again!"

"My God! Is that all I'm good for?" I asked, pretending to be angry.

"No, Babe, darling, don't take it that way." He continued to call me this endearing name for me from the start of our courtship. He stood up and gave me a hug. "It's only because I miss Tony whom we had

*He who grasps much, gets little.*

and then lost to his grandparents."

"But he's better off there, don't you think? He's getting the best care."

"Of course," Ping said. "I only hope he doesn't get so spoiled, he'd be unbearable."

"I don't think so. *Papá* has always been a disciplinarian. Look at me!" I said.

"So tell me. What is this earth-shaking surprise?"

I told him about Dr. Reyes's phone call inviting me to join his faculty in the new school.

"You mean you're going to work?" Ping asked, surprised.

"Yes, it's not a crime for a married woman to work. Wasn't I already working before we eloped? If I don't, I'll lose the chance to use what I've learned in school."

"I know. It's just that I always thought I would do all the working and earning in the family and the only thing you would do would be to attend to the house, make love to me, and take care of our children. . .because the way we are, there will be more!"

"But even if I'm working, I can still do all that. And I can help save for that dream house we plan to build."

"Okay, then, I won't stop you. We can give it a try. When do your classes start?"

"In two weeks if you'll let me. My two classes will be in the afternoon from 2:30 to 4:30. And the place is the Fajardo Building on Rizal Avenue, in front of the Ideal Theatre.

"Oh, good! After class you could walk over to the Savoy on Plaza Goiti and see our second show, and we can come home together for dinner."

"Perfect! Or I can do some shopping on the side while your show is going on,"

And that was our schedule until March of 1931 when the schools closed. Dr. Reyes gave me only one subject for the summer but it one hour and a half daily. That was still all right because I was through by four o'clock and I could go to the Savoy after that. According to Ping he rested between shows sleeping on the sofa back stage. There was a little rest area which served as a dining place too for the actors and all the others in the show.

During our frequent gatherings with the company I noticed that Mary, the pretty one, preferred Ping's company to the other men in the group and I teased him about it once. He said that it was because she was practicing her Spanish with him. Ping's mother was a Spanish teacher before she got married and her children grew up speaking the language. That was why we often spoke the language at home, more than the native Tagalog.

"Babe sweetheart, no one can come up to your exceptional qualities. So don't even think I would give her the time of day."

One afternoon in May, classes were dismissed earlier because of a convocation where a prominent speaker was to address the whole school.

I bought some *siopao*, *balut*, and other snacks, and put them in a bag for the company. According to their schedule, they would be resting after their first show. There was nobody in the sitting room where Ping usually rested so I decided to go to Mary's room. The door was not locked so I opened it. What I saw hit me like a bolt of lightning. Mary and my husband were in an unmistakably compromising position. Only an idiot would not have known what they were doing. At first, I was stunned, not wanting to believe what I was seeing in front of me. My next reaction, however, was one of disgust then anger. I remember throwing the bag of delicacies on the sofa, closing the door with a bang, and running down the hall and out of the building. I could not bear the enormity of my husband's deceit. All I wanted to do was to get as far away as possible from where they were.

I do not remember now how I got home. I could not erase what I saw from my mind and it was torture. I felt as though I had been stabbed, and I wanted to scream. The pain was so real. Then I just felt so numb that the tears would not come. I told the maid that I was going to be in my room but under no circumstances was I to be disturbed, not even by my husband. I locked the door and sat on the bed shaking, wondering what I was to do next. I contemplated leaving Ping, but thought of our son who did not even know what it was like to have the care of a mother and father and that was when the tears came. Ping came home earlier than usual and when I did not open the door to his furious knocking he used his key to come in. He tried to explain the situation that led to the scene that I saw. I refused to listen to what he had to say. I simply told him that I had made up my mind to leave him as soon as possible

I called my father and told him what had happened and that I had decided to leave Ping as soon as I could. *Papá* told me to wait until he got to Manila. He came the very next day and while Ping was at work he talked to me. He said that it was not always the fault of the man. He said that what most likely happened was that here was this beautiful, enticing woman with her seductive body and alluring movements sending waves of attraction. Ping had to see it show after show holding back with all his force the strong need to satisfy his lust. *Papá* told me that what happened was bad; it was a sin; it was everything despicable. But it did not lessen one bit Ping's great love for me. "You did not marry a saint, for if you did, you wouldn't have run away from us to go to where his great passion awaited you Again I will repeat that his misbehavior was uncalled for. But listen to me, Sarah, this does not lessen all the love he has for you. This is the first, and I hope the last time you have to go through this. But I have seen the two of you together and I know that he loves you, as much as you love him. He adores you, and sometimes, it is not easy for a man to be in love with an idol."

It seemed unbelievable that my own father defended and tried to lessen the gravity of Ping's fault. He asked me to understand it from Ping's point of view.

"Why don't I go with you to Santa Cruz and live there forever?" I asked as the tears started again.

"No, *hija*, you are looking at this incident out of proportion to what it really is. Remember that you were married with God's blessing, and every time he comes to you as a husband he does it with genuine love. That other act was merely giving in to a base human desire. So find it in your own love to forgive him."

*Papá*'s words quieted my anger, but I still could not find it in my heart to forgive Ping. He had hurt me. I trusted him with all my heart, and he had abused that trust.

Seeing that I was still tense and unforgiving, *Papá* said, "I will tell your mother to come here and bring Tony."

The next day Mama came with Tony and my father left for his job in Santa Cruz. As soon as I held my son in my arms I decided I could not leave this piece of my heart without a mother and father. He was almost ten months then and had learned to say "Mama" and "Papa" very sweetly. Every time I heard him say it my heart would jump with joy and I resolved that he would grow up with both parents loving him.

My mother-in-law also came and invited Tony and me to San Pedro Makati so *Tía* Nena could see him. We went with her while my mother took care of the house and the meals for Ping and Onching.

"I will never share my bed with him again," I told my mother-in-law.

"No, *hija*, don't say that. It's the worst thing you could do because you will be driving him to other women with his need. What Ping did with that woman was merely to satisfy a human urge. It was entirely without love, not the way that it is when he does it with you."

"Have you had a similar experience? "I asked her point blank.

"Not only once!" she said. "After the first one I did not want to die; I wanted to kill!" she said, and I laughed because I could see her doing it too.

"Is this part and parcel of marriage then? And did you continue sleeping with him after those times?"

"Of course. How do you think I got the six brothers and sisters of your husband?"

She was quite a woman, my mother-in-law! I was quiet after that talk with her, knowing that I wanted very much to have more children with Ping. But I was still terribly hurt by what I had seen and was not sure I was ready to forgive Ping.

During our three-day visit with *Tía* Nena she also sat with me one evening while everyone else was playing with Tony in another part of the house.

"*Naku*, if you had known your *Tío* Dado—her husband had died before Ping and I were married—you would have realized how much I had suffered sharing him with other women. He was handsome like your husband and very gracious in his dealings with all, especially with women. Men like the flattery and attention that women pay them. And it becomes a contest between the conqueror and the conquered. But your *Tío* never neglected his family. More important, he never failed to show me how much he loved me.'

After that talk I realized that the horrible scene I had witnessed was part and parcel of male-female relationships. Happy was the wife who had such a hold over her husband that he never wandered away from her arms. In my case, I had neglected to read the fine print before giving myself to him body and soul. Those allegations of women much older than I and far more experienced in bringing up their husbands and children, in a way softened the great load of sorrow in my heart. But it was hard for me to accept and even harder still to forgive.

When we arrived from San Pedro Makati that evening Ping was already home. He had been there since six o'clock, their second show having been cancelled due to a fire in the vicinity of the theater. He grabbed Tony right away and started playing with him on the bed, talking to the boy but really to make me hear what he was saying.

"Your *Lolo* talked to me on the phone for one hour."

"*Lolo?*" asked the boy. He really adored his grandfather.

"He is in Santa Cruz and is expecting you in a day or so,"

At which I asked, "They are going to Santa Cruz with my son? Does this mean I cannot hold my son anymore?"

"Well, ask him with whom he wants to be," teased Ping.

"Tony, with whom do you want to be, with Papa and Mama or with *Lolo* and *Lola?*"

"With *Lolo* and *Lola*" he answered unashamedly. pointing to my mother.

"Okay, one more year and you come back here, huh?"

And he smiled and said, "Yes".

After they left, Ping sat on my bed. He took my hand and kissed it and I could not withdraw it because my heart really craved for the warmth of his touch.

"Sweetheart," he said, "Please let me explain how I came to be in that position when you opened the door."

"NO!" I cut him short. "I want to erase all of that from my memory."

"Okay, darling, all I want to tell you is that it was not my idea..."

"STOP IT!" I screamed.

"Then let me show you how much I love you right now."

"No, no!" and I turned away from him.

But I was only fooling myself for my whole body ached for him to touch me. Ping did not stop caressing me and after a little while, we were lovers once more.

As I think of it even now after so many decades, I continue to wonder what unexplainable attraction he had for me.

## Chapter Nine

There were a few more turbulent days in our life, but Ping and I decided to bring our relationship back to where it was when we first started—loving, trusting, and joyous—with our emotions well under control, and always conscious of our sacred duties as man and wife and parents. What bound us strongly was our common desire to have another child. Our first one, Tony, had become a sacrificial offering to my parents, to assuage the pain we caused them by our hasty jump into marriage. We wanted another one whom we would love and indulge in a way that most new parents do with their first born.

After that month of May that left us with frayed emotions and brought me so much heartache, I realized that Ping was really making an effort to show me how much he cared for me and he did this in so many ways. I appreciated that and loved him for it. And I always kept in mind what my father had told me: no wife should go into a marriage expecting that she has married a saint. In time the pain healed but even the tiniest wound leaves a scar, and it was hard for me to forget and forgive what I had so graphically seen. Nevertheless, Ping was as considerate and gentle as he was during our courtship. He no longer went around with a hangdog look and his sense of humor was back. We began to tease each other once again, and there were many loving moments.

Then in June came the beginning of the new school year. On the third day of the month I got a copy of the tentative schedule of classes together with my proposed assignment. I had been given the choice of either morning or afternoon classes. After considering our daily activities in relation to Ping's job and mine, I decided to teach in the afternoon for that would allow us to come home together. This school year I was given six classes—two for English and four for Spanish.

That would bring in better earnings. I was also happy with an afternoon schedule because it would give me the whole morning to do what had to be done in the house and supervise the maid in doing the cleaning and laundry, and other chores.

One of my concerns was preparing the clothes I would wear for my job. My teaching included Saturday afternoons so I did not have time to do any sewing. But it was a chance to earn as much as Ping in his present job. My happy expectations made me push to the background, the cruel incident that almost broke our marriage too soon. One other comfort came from Carmen, a chorus girl who claimed to be distantly related. She said that since that fateful day, Ping hardly talked with the performers but kept to himself most of the time.

With the opening of classes I was really in good spirits. I would be making some money from my own efforts and using what I had learned in school. Yet somehow my body didn't seem to be responding to everything I had planned to do. For some reason, I was feeling sluggish. Trying to figure out what was wrong with me, I realized that I had missed my monthly period.

"Oh Lord," I said to myself, "I could be pregnant again!" and I had mixed feelings. Ping and I had talked so many times of how we wanted another baby, that was true, but why did it have to come now when I had such high hopes of earning big money? I knew that I could not be wiser than He who had given me the first one.

I gave Ping the news as soon as he came home that evening, and he was wild with joy,

"I hope it is a girl this time," he said. "It just has to be a girl!"

"I will pray very hard to the Blessed Mother of Lourdes," I said, amused but glad with his reaction.

Then I remembered what Nenita Paredes made me promise when we were still students at the UP—that my first girl should be named after her.

Ping said it was too early to rejoice. We had to be sure first that it was really a pregnancy.

Dr. Kabigting happened to be out of town that evening so we called on Dr. Jose Genato Sr. instead. He said that the mere absence of the monthly period was not a sure indication of pregnancy. We had to wait some more time.

"It is because we want another baby so badly," Ping explained.

"Well." said Dr. Genato, "Keep working on it constantly," he teased.

So we dropped the subject and decided to work on it for another month.

On the second Monday of June, Ping helped me to prepare for school. He had no rehearsal that morning so we were through quickly. When we got to the university, we found it already full of students who had enrolled previously some who were just coming in. My classes were not large, just like the ones I had when I eloped. I knew I was going to enjoy teaching them. That afternoon, Ping picked me up after the second show and we went home together.

By the end of June I was dead sure I was pregnant. I had those feelings of an upset stomach, and discomfort that I had felt with my first baby. Ping was openly joyous with expectation. He was once again concerned that I do the right thing for the baby and myself, and even suggested that I quit teaching as soon as I was sure.

"No," I said. "Definitely not. That is pure nonsense. At least my work keeps my mind off my nausea and discomfort."

"But you may miscarry. You are never still, you move too much," he cautioned.

"I do not!" I retorted. "In school there is an elevator to the second floor and I have my classes only on that one floor."

I informed Dr. Reyes about my condition and he was very happy that I would have another baby. He said he would help me pray it would be a girl.

Ping was so happy and sometimes, we were like two foolish children. After supper in the evening he would ask: "Which bed this time? Yours or mine?"

And when I usually said, "Mine," he would say, "Are you sure it will be a girl if we do it there?"

"Most likely," I would say, and then he would add:

"I think you're right because with Tony it was mostly on mine."

It is a wonder what having a baby does for expectant parents. Our relationship was at a new height, and I was in awe of the way we enjoyed loving and working hard, and praying it would be a girl.

Time rolled by so quickly that I did not feel it going by because I was so busy changing the decor in the nursery and bassinet from blue to pink. I even got a receiving blanket that was pink all over.

"And suppose it happens to be a boy? What will you do?" my mother asked. She was advising that I use a more neutral color like cream which would be suitable for either sex.

"No," I said firmly. "The Blessed Mother of Lourdes has never yet disappointed me."

I knew that my friend Nenita Paredes was praying too because of the pact we had made before graduation.

In school Dr. Reyes asked me whether I had already decided when I would go on my maternity leave. I told him I could still teach until the Christmas break. I was not having any problems carrying this baby. Except for the increase in weight and at times a little tired feeling, my pregnancy developed very normally. The only difference I noted was that the baby was heavier than Tony.

Sometime in October during the mid-semester break Ping told me he was going to tell me something that he should have told me long before then. He made such a serious introduction that I started to get anxious. I told him to tell me after dinner and we could at least try to enjoy our meal.

When we finished with dessert, we went to the sofa and I told him that I was ready to hear what he had to say. He told me that during the crisis when I wanted to leave him, my father offered him a deal. *Papá* had told him that he understood how he came to be in that situation with Mary because he was with her almost all day and whether consciously or not, he was heroically controlling the natural reaction of men who find themselves in such circumstances. He suggested that he play only in the first show and that he hire and train another piano-player for the second show. Then he could use his free time to study in the school where I was teaching and finish the course in Accounting that he abandoned for jazz. Of course he would lose his pay for the second show but my father promised to give him that plus one hundred pesos for other expenses related to his course. Besides that, my mother also had assured us that we would get two or three sacks of rice, one sack of sugar, and plenty of eggs and chickens for our meals. Ping said he agreed to that in principle but he first wanted to discuss it with me,

When I heard that I jumped up and hugged him so tight he said I would take all the breath out of him. I had to laugh. "You see, my father is an angel, isn't he?"

"I hope I deserve all this benevolence. Really!" Ping answered.

"Of course you do! And, oh so much more. Then you can have a degree and you can apply for jobs other than those that have to do with music. I tell you my father is made of gold."

I called my father immediately and thanked him for giving my husband a chance at a college degree.

"That is a double-edged sword, *hija*," he said. "Give him a qualification for jobs other than music and take him away from strong temptations to sin." So Ping enrolled in only two subjects—Accounting I and Economics I. He would have to slowly get used to a student's life after being away from it for almost five years.

Just when we thought things had started to look up, our life path took on another turn unexpectedly. On the 18th of December, 1931, Ping's father died suddenly of a heart attack, leaving a widow, six children and a sister-in-law to fare for themselves in uncharted waters.

Ping's mother had never bothered about the income or other problems of the family. Her husband had never wanted her to worry about anything aside from being a mother to their children the youngest of whom, was a girl, just five years old. So Ping, being the oldest, had to stop his studies in order to attend to the funeral and to straighten out matters regarding his father's estate.

Don Leocadio Joaquin was a prominent lawyer, one whom people called "*abogado de campanilla*" in those days. He rubbed elbows with the high and mighty in government and politics and had a large clientele of commercial giants. Ping's godfather was Manuel L. Quezon, the first president of the Republic of the Philippines, but he became that to Ping when he was still a governor of his province, Tayabas, later named Quezon, after him. The godparents of Ping's siblings also came from the roster of high government officials and prominent figures in Philippine history.

In his later years, however, Leocadio began to slow down because of the little illnesses that accompany the process of aging, to the extent that he could no longer be as active in the practice of his profession. As a result, his income began to dwindle.

*Tía* Nena who came after my mother-in-law among the sisters, presided at the meetings discussing the funeral arrangements and the future of the large family. The house would have to be sold not earlier than March of the following year so as not to disturb the schooling of the younger ones. There were only two girls, Generosa whose pet name was Nene, was finishing high school at the *Colegio de Santa Isabel*, and Carmen, the youngest, was only five years old. All the relatives came to the help of Mama Salome, my mother-in-law, and offered their services to ease the problems the family was facing.

It was agreed that after March, Enrique, whom everyone called Titong, and much later Ike, and Walfrido, whose pet name was Freddie, would live with *Tía* Dionisia and *Tío* Perico, cousins of my father-in-law, who had a big bakery in Pasay, a small town near the city

The other two, Augusto, or Gusty, as everyone called him, and Adolfo, called Adolf, were to go with a cousin in San Pedro, Makati, where they would just help with some household chores after school. Nene, *Tía* Naty, Mama's younger sister, would stay together in another house that they would rent after they sold the present one.

I remember the meeting where the separation of the siblings was decided and my heart broke upon hearing the way they would all be separated. I had known the exuberance of Ping's family every time they were all together and felt the warmth of all especially when Mama Salome would serve the dishes for which she had become famous.

Ping and I would take care of Mama's household expenses in the meantime. I was very willing to help Ping with this and my parents understood that. In their subtle way, my parents never sent goods directly to Mama Salome, but they would more than double what they were sending us so we could then give the rest to Mama Omeng.

Then, as if Fate was testing us to see how much more we could take of life's trials, Ping received a very tempting offer to take a band and play for 10 or twelve months in a big hotel in Surabaya, on the island of Java. He had to think about it for several days because he didn't want to leave me knowing the baby was due during the time he would be away. And yet the amount he would earn would cover what he would have to give his mother and more, so he would have something to put aside for a rainy day. I told him it was all right. This was our second baby. I would already know what to do when the time came.

Convinced that it would be all right, Ping got his former band at the Army and Navy Club and added one or two more members. He left his band at the Polo club to a trusted friend to manage for him while he was gone.

*Mamá* offered to be in Manila. as soon as Ping left on New year's Day. It broke my heart to see him go but I was able put on a brave face and kiss him goodbye without any tears. He was doing it to help shoulder the responsibilities of his two families and I vowed to help him do that.

"Send me pictures of my pretty daughter as soon as she is born," were his last instructions. "Stay strong," he told me and after telling me he loved me with his life, and kissing me good-bye, he was gone.

On the 18th day of February, 1932 I gave birth to an eight-and-a-half pound girl who gave a louder and longer wail than Tony.

Of course my sworn *comadre*, Lourdes, who made me promise to name my first daughter after her when we were still back at the UP, was there to see me through my birth pangs. It was she who readily reported that the baby's name, Lourdes, as we had agreed upon, would be on the birth certificate. I had called her the night before when I felt the first contractions, and like the first time *Ate* Elena was in attendance. My cousin, the doctor, said I would probably deliver about 2:00 the following morning but my Nenita, did not wait that long and came much earlier at 11:00 that evening.

Ping was jubilant when he heard it was an easy delivery. According to one of his men in the orchestra, Ping passed out bags of chocolate candy all around the hotel saying his wife had just given birth to the future Miss.Philippines. He wanted to make a quick visit home just to see me and the baby but I told him it would be foolish to do that, a useless expense. I would take as many pictures as I could and send them to him.

I wanted to go back teaching in the summer of 1932 but my father was against it saying he would just give me the money I would earn. He said my daughter needed my attention more than ever since Ping was away.

*Mamá* stayed until Nenita was three months old and everything was running smoothly. She was able to get a good *yaya* for the baby, a spinster daughter of one of my grandfather's tenants from San Miguel, Bulacan. The moment I saw her, I knew I could entrust my daughter to her. She was neat, very patient and dedicated to her job. Before she left *Mamá* suggested that I look around for a bigger place to move to as our apartment had become too small for all of us.

During the summer I spent my time making clothes for myself because again I had become much smaller than when I was pregnant. When some of my friends found out that I made my own dresses they asked me if I would be willing to sew for them, and, of course, pay me for the work. They insisted I made better dresses and had better taste when it came to style so they brought their fabrics to me and I suddenly found myself busy with a new business.

This gave me an idea. My mother-in-law had moved to Pasay, then a small town just outside of Manila. They chose that place because two of her boys were with *Tía* Dionisia the owner of the bakery where the boys lived and worked. I could live there and have a dress shop and earn a little more. My sister-in-law, Nene, who also loved to sew, could help me and earn a little too.

My father gladly approved, so we moved into an apartment called an *accesoria*. These were two-story apartments with a long empty space at the opening of the ground floor often used as a store or living room. There was a partition separating that long area from a room that could be used as a kitchen cum dining room. Next to it was the bath area. Upstairs were three bedrooms and a bath

My father brought the farm truck to help us move and four farm hands who carried what furniture and equipment we had. By the end of the day, we were in our new place.

I chose to teach in the afternoon so I could oversee the preparation of the baby's bottles and bath and also the cooking of our meals. After I was left to teach, Nene, my sister-in-law supervised all the activities in the house and the shop. In the evening after we had dinner I cut some of the dresses that had to be finished first so Nene could sew them in the morning.

We had a good steady flow of customers especially when there were parties or on the days before holidays. Sometimes, Nene and I had to work until midnight to finish dresses that were needed for the next day. But I was very happy because I was earning much more than I had expected.

I wrote Ping all about this and he said he was very proud of me and told me how much more he loved me for it. But once burned, twice curious, and there were times when I was tempted to ask if there was some woman there who could be filling his "human needs". I always checked, though, not wanting to sour such loving conversation. I believed I had matured and I decided that as long as he did not give me any disease, I would not bring up his one-time infidelity by asking tasteless questions.

During that time in 1932 we were so busy we needed another 12 hours of the day. We had so many customers and we could not be lax in the quality of our work because our customers expected the best. At one time we forgot that we had a baby to care for. The baby's *yaya* was helping us press the newly finished garments one afternoon when it started to rain very hard. All of a sudden she dropped the iron and ran upstairs exclaiming "*Susmariosep!*" I ran after her to find out what was happening. She remembered that the baby was asleep and the windows were open so there would be fresh air in the room. By the time we got to Nenita, she was in her bed next to the window drenched to the skin.

"My God!" I shouted, and grabbed her. I wrapped her in a big towel and quickly gave her a warm sponge bath. Then I gave her the bottle and called my cousin, a doctor to ask what more I should do. She told me to rub her chest and back with Mentholatum and watch for any signs of a fever later on. I held her until she fell asleep and I put her in her warm bed and told Idang, the nursemaid to feel if she had a temperature every half hour.

When Ping called the next day to ask about his little princess I did not tell him about the incident because I knew that if I did, I probably would have been given a long distance sermon and told to give up all the sewing I was doing. Besides, Nenita didn't seem to have suffered from her experience.

Our customers increased way beyond our expectations because the wives of the US Army officers in Fort Mc Kinley learned about my shop from the Filipino band there and they flocked to our place like bees to a beehive. The Manila Polo Club where most of them went to dine or play games was in the outskirts of Pasay and it was very convenient for them to come and have their gowns made by us. By September we were virtually swamped with so many orders I had to ask *Tía* Naty and even Mama Salome at times to come and help us sew buttons or do the hems or iron the finished pieces.

Then one day in October my father came to have lunch with us and see his new granddaughter, He said he had a wonderful surprise for me.

"Really?" I asked. "Is it for me or for the baby?"

"For the whole family," he said happily "I will tell you after lunch."

After lunch he could no longer hold back the surprise he mentioned earlier. He told me that he had bought a house in San Juan del Monte, as it was called then. He did not say that it was for me but he insinuated that we could live there first. He felt he was going to be assigned to Rizal province whose capital is Pasig just outside Manila, and they could move there with us. Not with us really because he was already building a smaller apartment next to it where he and *Mamá* would stay. The house was to be where Ping and I would live with our growing family.

I told him it was very thoughtful of him to invite us to live there, but also said that I wanted to discuss this with Ping first. Besides I was doing very good business where we lived and at the same time, I was even helping my in-laws earn some money.

When Ping called I told him about the house and how *Papá* expected us to live there. Ping said it was all right with him, but asked to put off any move until he got back just before Christmas that year.

I could not stop thinking why all this had to come when I was earning so much in my present home and business. I was not resentful for it meant that we would no longer be renting but would have a house of our own. But I did regret losing the business. On the other hand, I also felt that I could not be wiser than the Lord. I believed that He would surely guide my actions.

*Papá* seemed to sense that I was not too happy about his buying the house in San Juan because I took his surprise without much excitement. I received it rather calmly, he said, while he was expecting me to be overjoyed. He used to call me the "girl of the superlatives" because I could never hide my feelings, not with him anyway. When I wanted something and he got it for me, I would always jump at him and hug him while saying thank you. When he said that, I told him that I was already an old married woman with two children so maybe I had changed.

The truth was that I would have to close my dress shop which was bringing in so much money. I knew *Papá* did not like it when he saw us with a big pile of dress materials to sew. Besides that, I still kept up with my teaching and also had a small baby to worry about. He had remarked when he saw me that I had lost some weight and my hair was not as well groomed as I used to fix it before I had the baby. I knew that in San Juan it would have been useless for me to open a shop because at that time it was still just a little hill town.

Ping was pleased that I would not have to worry about rent and other household expenses because my mother would take care of those. But he sensed that I was more excited about the sewing and the money that it brought in. He told me to thank *Papá* and tell him that he was all for it. He also reminded me to tell *Papá* that if it was all right, he would like to hold off any move until after he arrived on the second week of December. Then we could move after three of us had our birthdays—mine, Ping's and Nenita's.

So, I started refusing new customers because I wanted to have time to prepare for Ping's arrival and Christmas. I made some pretty covers and cushions for the furniture downstairs and draperies for the bedrooms upstairs. The baby's room was the prettiest of all. It was in different shades of soft pink and very soft beige. Then I got Nenita a charming set consisting of a pink dress, cap and booties with a sweet little cape to match,

Nene and I decorated a small Christmas tree which Onching had cut from *Tía* Dionisia's garden. It looked beautiful with the little angel on top and Nenita loved to touch the ornaments.

We met Ping at the airport and he went straight to Nenita and grabbed her from the nursemaid even before he kissed me. My mother-in-law and *Tía* Naty were there too.

We went for dinner at a Japanese restaurant since Ping said he had had enough of Chinese cooking. He and the band had stopped in Hongkong for four days so this evening, he wanted something different.

'And how is my big Babe, my sweetheart?' he came to me and gave me a noisy kiss on the cheek.' After looking me over and holding me close, he asked, "And what did you do to lose so much weight? Some people will think we're starving you."

"Ah, but I'm very happy because I am sought after and earning a lot of money," I calmly answered.

"What do you mean? You're earning enough with your teaching, aren't you?"

"It is the joy of doing something creative and for which I'm appreciated."

"But you have brought two beautiful babies into the world in less than three years. Isn't that accomplishment enough, sweetheart?"

"Well, with some help from you!" I countered. And everyone laughed.

We hardly slept at all that night. It seemed so strange to feel somebody close to me again. And we had so many stories to swap, but we had to get used to each other's presence once more. Even our giving to each other's pleasure seemed so strange and different.

The next day both of us slept late. Ping said it was probably the difference in time from the other countries that did it, but I believed it was because we had missed each other's warmth for a long time and the need to hold on to each other had become a necessity.

When my mother-in-law came after breakfast the next day she remarked, "I think you are handsomer than before. Some girls must have been crazy about you."

"NO, Ma," Ping was emphatic. I always showed them my wedding ring and they left me alone when they realized I was non-negotiable."

"But there really wasn't any need for negotiation, was there?" I asked, half in jest.

"Well, not really...just for the fun of it at times, which never amounted to anything."

For some reason, his answer hit me hard so I quickly changed the subject afraid that the conversation would turn sour.

"I think I heard the baby cry, didn't you? Is it time for her bottle?" I asked Idang, the baby's nursemaid.

"Yes, I have it right here. I'm just warming it a little." And with that she ran upstairs quickly followed by Ping who wanted to feed his daughter.

We had a lovely Christmas. Everyone including *Tía* Dionisia and *Tío* Perico had little gifts from Hongkong that Ping brought back. We had finished our sewing commitments for Christmas and the New Year so we started packing for the move to San Juan.

After the holidays Ping went to the Manila Polo Club to get what was due him in his absence and to see how his band was doing. He was informed that a new vaudeville company was playing at another movie house and whether he would be interested even though it's director was not his friend, Adolfo. Ping dismissed it saying he did not want to play for another such company because he was going to enroll that summer and finish what he left when his father died.

I was very happy when he told me this. It seemed that he had become more serious about considering the future, maybe because he already had two growing children. He knew he could earn much working with Adolfo who had many shows for the elite Smiles and Bachelor Clubs. In addition, he had two students who came to him to learn how to play jazz. So he was not altogether without any earnings. Also, moving to San Juan meant we did not have to think of any rent. Even our daily expenses were small because of what we got from the farm. By then, I was also teaching full time once again. So who could have blamed me for feeling that I was on cloud nine.

One thing kept nagging me though. Our love life was not as intensely ecstatic as it was before the babies came and Ping seemed to enjoy playing with his daughter more than spending time with me. It's true that I was teaching full time and he was studying and both of us were busy, but I continued to miss the closeness that was ours before he left. I thought all the time that absence was supposed to make the heart grow fonder. I felt that way, but Ping did not seem to know the meaning of that adage. But I did not want to make it an issue, so I just chose to think that we had started to become an old married couple and no longer sought nor needed the fire we knew in the early days of our marriage.

After school in March, 1933, we moved to our new house in San Juan. I felt sad about closing my shop. I missed the excitement of rushing to finish dresses and stimulating my creativity to design clothes especially suited to a particular client. My mother-in-law was even sadder to see us go but I assured her that we would visit her frequently and she would still get the little financial aid we were giving her. Being in San Juan made it inexpensive for us as there was no rent to pay and my father said he would take care of the other expenses like electricity, water bills and telephone since they lived in the same compound..

Everyone in the family voted against my teaching that summer. Ping, however, enrolled in the two subjects he had left when his father died. At times he would drive over and see his mother to bring her farm produce and leave her the money she needed for the week. In the afternoons, he would work with Adolfo's groups.

When he made the decision to work with Adolfo in the afternoon, I was a bit disappointed. I somehow thought that afternoons belonged to us so we could have time to be together by ourselves and with the baby. I felt that Ping had really changed in the eleven months that he was away. But I chose to think that he really wanted to earn more money to satisfy his own feeling of self-respect.

I kept myself busy with the decor of the new house. It was a fairly large one with a covered porch that served as the family room where games were played and songs were sung among the young and old. Next to it was the big living room with large, comfortable furniture and the dining area where a huge one-piece round table was in the center with ten comfortable chairs around it. There were three big bedrooms opening onto the side of the dining room. Then there was a roomy kitchen. on one side of which was a covered bridge that led to a fairly large efficiency apartment for my parents. Under this apartment was a garage for three cars. The basement of the big house could also be utilized as living quarters, should this be necessary. In a corner of the back garden was a cabin that served as the dirty kitchen.

At first, I was overwhelmed by the size of the house because it meant that lots of drapery and pillows had to be sewn, but I told myself that this would keep me busy enough so I wouldn't brood over my cooling relationship with my husband.

I was quire sure something was bothering him though because once or twice I would catch him in deep thought and even when I spoke to him, he would not answer me.

"A penny for your thoughts," I once said as I held his arm.

"Oh, sorry, sweetheart," he said startled.

"Is something wrong? You seem preoccupied," I said.

"I was just wondering how I could earn more to at least equal what you will be earning this June," was his reply.

"But why worry about that?" I asked. "We'll be living practically free of all payments. *Papá* will take care of the other household expenses and my mother will send the staples from the farm."

"But that's what this is all about!" His voice rose a decibel. "It's what embarrasses me. Even my mother's family is dependent on your resources."

"What is mine is yours and who cares who is dependent on whom?" And I gave him a tight hug and he hugged me back, but I felt that his heart was not really in it.

At the same time, I had a nagging feeling that there was more to his mood. It is amazing how a wife's intuition can be so sharp.

Sometime before Easter, I saw Totong, *Tía* Nena's son at a grocery store.

"How are you?" he greeted me. Then, hugging me, he remarked, "My, but you've lost weight."

"I've just been so busy with the move. That's why I am not teaching this summer," I told him.

"And who is that pretty relative of yours that Ping took to the airport one Sunday sometime ago?" He asked.

"What relative? And where was the girl going?"

"Ping told me she was going to Hongkong."

"Maybe you didn't hear right. I have no relatives in Hongkong." I said. "She probably was only a friend."

"Maybe. I was in a hurry and didn't pay much attention," he said, just before we parted.

So, I thought. That could have been the reason for all the coldness that I could not put a finger on, the absentmindedness that he claimed was about the family. I was terribly hurt. I thought that he had left all the temptation and sin behind him. I could not stop wondering how he could have found someone in Hongkong after a stay of only four days, and even have the gall to bring her here.

I remembered that particular Sunday when Totong saw him. It was when he told me he would have to work with his friend Adolfo López about a show.

When he came home that night, he brought some *siopao*, and *pansit* from a Chinese restaurant saying he remembered how much I loved Chinese food.

"Indeed." I said. "But not as much as you love Chinese women, I'm sure."

"Now where is that coming from?" he asked me.

"Didn't you take a pretty young girl to the airport and say that she was a relative of mine?"

"All right, since you brought it up let me tell you that when you caught me once not listening to your question it was because I was debating with myself if I should tell you the truth before you found it out. But I was a coward so I told you something else."

"All right, I'm ready to listen now. I think you should know that it will hurt me but I will not think of leaving you because we have two children now. And, unfortunately...for me...I happen to be fool enough to love you very much. That, Ping, will always be my cross here on earth."

Suddenly, he hugged me. Then he began, "I accepted the Hongkong job at the Peninsula Hotel because it would bring my group some big money for only four days. A fellow musician who had lived there for several years introduced me to this eighteen-year-old British-Chinese call girl, and even paid for her services. The girl, who was not yet too submerged in her profession took a fancy to me and on her own came here thinking I was single. I've been trying to send her back home for a week but she finally decided when I could not pay for her hotel and her money was gone that she should leave...But, Babe, sweetheart, she is no comparison to you at all."

"NO, she cannot compare with me at all because I am a fool."

"Babe, don't say that. Don't ever call yourself that." And he began to caress me but I was already too hurt to respond to such feigned sweetness.

Then he asked me if I wanted to eat the Chinese food he brought.

"You even have the gall to add insult to injury?" I retorted angrily.

That night he slept in my bed, holding me close, but we did not make love. I was just too upset to be anywhere near being responsive. I lay in his embrace but I did not sleep the entire night.

In the morning, I looked him straight in the eye and said, "Okay, Ping. Let's just get one thing straight. I want you to remember that every action has its corresponding reaction. Not that I'm planning on it, but if some day in the future I pay you back with the same coin, don't hold it against me."

Sarah Joaquin
*circa 1955*

Tony, Sarah, Porfirio (Ping) Joaquin,
Josefina (Jojo), Lourdes

Dr. Francisco Hernando with
wife Manuela *(only sister of Sarah)*
with children
Benny *(left)*, Eugenio *(behind)*,
and Marita

Balbino Yuson Kabigting,
Bobby, Sarah Joaquin
& Tony

Chita & Tony Joaquin

Marijean, Mikee, Bobby, Nico Joaquin

Gina & nephew Julian Joaquin

Cristina & Jowin Claudio

Jenny & Jay Joaquin with son Julian

Patrick & Lizza Osborn

Zinnia & Freddie de la Rosa
with
their sons Elijah, Noah

Fred and Josefina (Jojo) de la Rosa
with their sons
Dino, Freddie, Luis

Monica and Luis
with sons Diego, Marco, Mateo

Erica Roque, Lizanne Roque,
Lourdes (Nenita) Rasmussen, Sarah Joaquin

Anthony Roque & sister Erica

Martin & his mother
Sarah-Lee Flores

Joey & Flor Joaquin with son Jonathan

Lourdes & Norman Rasmussen, Chita & Tony Joaquin,
Flor Joaquin, Josefina de la Rosa, Joey Joaquin, Sarah Joaquin

## Chapter Ten

Life went on quite smoothly after that. I started the school year with a full time load of eight subjects: three in English, three in Spanish, and two in Voice and Diction. Dr. Reyes told me that they had just bought the Far Eastern College from the Maronilla brothers and we would have to move to a building on Azcarraga Street, now Claro M. Recto. It used to be a cigarette factory and repairs were being carried out to convert it into a school.

I was eagerly looking forward to the new building and the courses I was going to teach.in June. So once again, I looked over the clothes I would need for the coming school year. Surely with a full assignment I would hardly have any time at all to sew as I would be in school even on Saturdays.

I was not too worried about the new baby because Idang, the nursemaid, was very efficient and my mother was there most of the time as my father was temporarily assigned to the Department of Finance.

Ping was enrolled in only four subjects because he had to be with Adolfo most of the time. I was no longer concerned whether he stayed faithful or not having somehow convinced myself that I could not expect him to change and I might as well accept the fact that I just had to learn to share him with other women. Our lovemaking had become fewer and far between although in all honesty, I would have wanted it to happen more often. Nevertheless, I did not complain even though often times Ping's touches seemed so perfunctory. I always remembered what I was told as a bride, that a wife should never refuse her husband, and I never did.

But fate has her ways of fooling us mortals. As the school year was just starting, I began feeling out of sorts once more. My stomach seemed a bit upset as I went to classes on the first day. Once again, I noticed that I had missed my period. "Oh, no!" I thought unhappily, "I can't possibly be pregnant again." Sure enough, after I went to the doctor for tests, I found out I was carrying my third child. As he was with all my previous pregnancies, Ping was beside himself with joy.

"Good! I hope it's another girl," he said.

"Why do you want so many girls?" I asked him, laughing.

"Because if we get a boy, your mother will take him again," Ping quickly retorted.

Being pregnant was not any reason for me to reduce my assigned classes, and neither did I give up the extra-curricular activities that were placed under my charge. I organized two debating clubs, calling them the Cicero and Demosthenes Clubs and asked Dr. Gregorio Zaide to be the adviser of one while I took care of the other. I set up a group to be trained for dramatics and hoped that after I delivered my baby I would be able to present some plays. I promised the members that we would start staging plays the next school year. All this time I hoped and prayed that I would not be pregnant again.

In the meantime Dr. Reyes gave me the news that the Far Eastern University, which was the name the school was given, had bought the large piece of unused land where we would have to transfer within the next two years as the present school building was slated for demolition to give way for the Quezon Boulevard already under construction. This was good news to me as well.

Ping, too, came with another bit of information. He had been offered a contract in China, not in Hongkong but in some place near the border with Russia. He had quoted a very high price to the company thinking they would not take it up and he was told they would let him know in a few days.

Once more, my heart sank again. Again, he would not be around when I gave birth to my baby. He placated me saying that he wanted to save some money because by then, we would already have three children. It was better that we started to save up for their education as early as we could.

"Besides," he added." I learned my lesson after that affair in Hongkong. I assure you, Babe, it will never be repeated. I promise you that."

He may have meant it, but knowing him, I had my doubts. I knew his weakness well, and while I accepted his promise, I did not hold him to it. I had already faced the bitter reality before and I no longer had any illusions that he would stay faithful to me. The Company that had approached him came through and met his demands so not long after, Ping left and once again, it was my mother who filled the void.

That Christmas was not the round of preparations and excitement that usually came with the holiday. Ping had said he would not be back until April or May. His reason was that it was too far to travel and it was best to save the money. By that time, I had my own way of dealing with his promises. When one's trust so freely given at one time is lost, it is not easy to trust again. I might have been unfair to him by thinking this way, but I also felt it was not the money he was thinking of but the freedom to do as he wanted without being tied down by family obligations.

For the sake of my children, I had resolved to be brave and keep up the lively spirit of the season. I loved Ping and I missed him, but I would shake off my loneliness by throwing myself into my work with passion. I would cultivate the arts that I had learned and loved from childhood and that had been fostered at the *Centro*. And I decided then that if at some point Ping and I came to a parting of the ways I would hold on to my children.

The days passed very quickly and my pregnancy was no trouble at all. As with the previous one I stopped teaching during the Christmas break.

In the beginning of February, my sister, Nene, got maried to Dr. Francisco Hernando after an engagement of five years. I remember I was big with child when I made her wedding gown. They made their home in Santa Cruz where her husband was assigned as District Health Officer in Laguna.

My parents lived in their little apartment behind the house and their driver was always present so I knew there would be no problem with my going to the hospital when the time came. In the early afternoon of February 26, 1934, I felt a contraction. When I told my mother about it she made me take a shower. Then she called my father to take me to the hospital right away. *Mamá* knew how fast the birth would come once I had my labor pains. Sure enough, as we were entering the Philippine General Hospital, the pains started. A nurse came to meet us at the elevator with a wheelchair but she said I should walk instead as that would help the labor.

"Will you be responsible if my grandchild is born right here?" *Papá* asked her. Frightened, she quickly wheeled me to the delivery room. My cousin, the doctor, was out of town so another doctor was ready to receive me. They were putting me on the delivery table to prepare me for the doctor to take over when the baby came.

"Doctor, doctor! The baby! It's coming! I can't stop it," the nurse shouted as she grabbed a towel and received the seven-pound baby girl. By the time the doctor got to me, he only had to do the finishing touches.

I called Ping in Harbin and was told that the band was in Hongkong, playing at the Peninsula Hotel. The information was a stab in my heart. Somehow I knew he would be with that girl again. Once more, I could only console myself with the thought that I had the baby and if worse came to worst he would never have the children.

The baby was baptized Josefina Carmen, the latter name after her godmother Carmen, wife of Dr. Irineo Carlos, my cousin the dentist of the family. Idang, the *yaya* was overjoyed. Nenita was already two years old and while she loved to see her baby sister bathed and fed and taken to the garden, she was no longer a baby. Josefina was not as fussy as Nenita had been as an infant and Nenita insisted on calling her Baby.

When Baby was six months old, Ping came home. As he did with Nenita, he carried Baby around and danced with her. "So she will know I'm her father," he said. By then I no longer cared how he felt about me. I did not even ask him if he saw that girl there. Knowing him, I didn't think he could have been chaste that long.

**W**hen Ping arrived sometime about the end of July, most of the classes at the Far Eastern University had already moved to the make-shift building built on what used to be nothing but a wasteland. There were only a handful of us who had been there from the very beginning with Dr. Reyes and he made it clear that he was depending on us to show the ropes to the rest of the new faculty.

Changes were also taking place at home. For one thing, the children were growing up fast and it was time to start thinking of schooling, for Tony in particular. San Juan was starting to be a suburb where families with young children began to build their homes. Aurora Aquino, my former seatmate in three subjects who had become the second wife of then Senator Benigno Aquino, was among those who moved with her family to San Juan. They had three children, Benigno Jr. whom everyone called Ninoy, then Maur, who was Nenita's age, and Lupita who was just a bit older than Baby. When the Aquinos had settled in their beautiful home, Aurora called me and we chatted for a long time. Such calls eventually became a habit. Once in a while, Aurora would bring her children to our house and that was how the families became close friends.

In 1937, Ninoy and Tony, who was already staying with us, needed to go to a kindergarten school. Most of the good boys' schools were in Manila and that was too far from us. But there was St. Joseph's College, a girls' school, very near the Aquino house that admitted boys up to kindergarten. So we decided that Ninoy and Tony would start their schooling there. Worrying about where to send them for grade school would be dealt with when the time came.

When the boys were being enrolled, the Dutch sisters in St. Joseph said they could also enroll the girls in the nursery school or in kindergarten. My father was delighted but poor Baby would be left alone at home. The sisters said they also had a pre-nursery school. So Baby, too, was enrolled at St. Joseph. Everyday when she came home, I would ask her what she did in class and her answer always was, "Tomorrow no class."

After a year of schooling at St.Joseph's College, Ninoy and Tony had to go to a regular school for boys as the sisters no longer accepted boys beyond kindergarten, first grade at the most. Seeing that it was a problem that was bothering me, *Papá* bought me a house in the heart of Manila where there were already many schools. It was in the corner of San Rafael St and Arlegui, about two blocks away from Malacañang Palace.

On Morayta street which could be seen from one of our windows upstairs, there was the College of the Holy Ghost, now the Holy Spirit for girls, and right beside it was the San Beda College for boys. In front of San Beda was the *Centro Escolar* University which had moved from its old site in Azcarraga, now Claro M. Recto, and behind this was the Manila East High School. On San Rafael Street about two hundred yards from our house was La Consolacion College, and farther up the street was the San Sebastian College. The schooling of the children would be no problem. I was very happy because Tony was to be enrolled in San Beda and would stay with us five days a week. On Friday afternoons, his grandfather picked him up to spend the weekend with them. The arrangement suited me fine. The girls went to the Holy Ghost College. In San Juan the girls were picked up by bus; here they just walked to the school in a matter of ten minutes.

My house in Arlegui was an old one, one of those houses built in the latter part of the Spanish time using the best materials available in the country. The Philippines has special kinds of hard wood that can last several centuries and the house was built of these. It stood modestly, representing the architectural style of the old days, which offered two independent household quarters on two different floors. The top floor had three big bedrooms, a spacious living-dining room area and a conveniently designed kitchen with a big table in the middle for various household activities. The old-fashioned bathroom had both a tub and shower and was large enough to include a dressing room. The living quarters had a master's bedroom at the rear end of the building, large enough for a set of twin beds with a night table in between. The room also had a large armoire and dresser and in one corner was an easy chair with a footstool.

My days were busy. In the morning and early afternoon I did my teaching and in the evening after supper I would cut or sew uniforms for the girls. Once I had done that, I redecorated the house, giving vent to my artistic leanings and my sewing skills. When it came to the children's room, I went all out. I bought two hanger-drawer wardrobes for kids and painted them soft beige all over. Then I painted on each hangar door a young girl with a wide-brimmed hat holding a bouquet of flowers. For Tony I painted a smiling boy dressed in a baseball uniform with a baseball cap and swinging a bat

When my father saw what I had done, he lost no time in buying three beds: two identical beds with detachable safety rails and a bigger blue one, obviously for Tony. This third room could also be a guest room as Tony was not with us during the weekends.

The master bedroom was in simple aqua and soft orange. I knew Ping's favorites were soft colors. Once these were done, I gave all my attention to the three living room doorsI was happily occupied doing over the house, which I thought, looked very good. It even entered my mind that I could go into the business of home decoration, except, of course, that I really loved my teaching.

On the first floor, just below the master bedroom was the room I referred to as the bachelor's quarters. It was a complete unit with its own entrance from the street and its own bathroom with a shower. I had invited two cousins of mine: Gerardo de Leon on the side of my father, and a lawyer, Leandro Sevilla, on the side of my mother, to occupy that room. Gerardo whom we called Adong was a working student in FEU and at home acted as my handyman helping me with the painting and hanging up the draperies.

*I*n the meantime some buildings were already built in the newly acquired land by FEU that would sufficiently house three institutes and two high schools. For some reason that I never understood, a Girls High School and a Boys High School were put in along with the Institute of Accounting Business and Finance, the Institute of Education and the Institute of Arts. I was in the largest building, one that held all the preparatory courses for law, medicine, and nursing.

With a larger and more permanent place, I organized a public debate for two clubs and compelled all pre-law students to become members. I also submitted to the Department of Education, a curriculum making Radio Broadcasting a college course instead of its original status as a vocational one. My coup de grace, however was, the establishment of the FEU Drama Guild. Sometime in the second semester of that school year, we presented the first full-length play *Call Me Mike*. I knew that my forte was not in directing but in acting so I asked two former UP actor-directors to help me. I acted as adviser. The FEU

Drama Guild went all out for that production and not having our own auditorium as yet, we had to get one of the two Rufino theatres on Rizal Avenue for the venue. Dr. Reyes passed a memo that all Full-time faculty members should go and see it.

The play was received with such resounding success that Dr. Reyes invited the cast and crew of the production and the faculty to a late dinner at the Ideal Hotel across the street. Most of the papers headlined the big success of a relatively newly-formed group and my name was mentioned several times as a future director who should bear watching.

When Ping read about it he gave me a big kiss on the cheek saying:

"Hey, congratulations! I have a very theatrical wife."

"And you know what?" I remarked. "Dr. Reyes already promised me that the plans for the big building include a real theater, one that will have everything that a professional theater has."

"Well, isn't that something! From the president no less," he remarked.

By that time, Ping had already completed all the requirements for a Bachelor of Science in Accounting and Finance. However he asked me not to force him to join the graduation exercises in cap and gown because that would only underscore the fact that he did not have a degree when he married me. After the graduation ceremonies, we had a private lunch with my in-laws, my parents and of course my three children.

I did not know what my father did but in three weeks, he brought us the news that Ping had a job as cashier in the Manila Port Terminal that was to be run by Don Enrique Razon, a very influential man in the government of Manual Quezon. The truth was that the Commonwealth President, Manuel Quezon, who was Ping's godfather did not even know Ping had been hired. When Pres. Quezon visited their offices several months later, Ping was already working there. All the employees had been instructed on how to greet the President and everyone was surprised that Ping kissed the President's hand instead of shaking it. The President hollered to Captain Razon in Spanish, "Why did you not tell me this boy is here?" And Razon answered "I did not know he was related to you at all."

Ping's job brought me both relief and joy. There would be no more musical shows where Ping had to gaze at the semi-nude bodies of women of questionable repute. At first Ping was not very happy. Music had been his life for so long and working in an office was new to him. My father had a ready remedy for that too. He assigned one of his employees in the office of the provincial treasurer to mentor Ping for two months with extra pay so Ping could understand the job and do it well. So now Ping had a semi-government position instead of a fly-by-night show that was very temporary. I felt that our life would now have some stability.

At FEU, I was also very busy with eight subjects to teach, actors to train and plays to present. On top of these were parties and dinners that the faculty was expected to attend. I was always with my colleagues in the Institute of Arts, most of them with doctorates, masters and specialties, and Ping did not relish attending it with me. He said he would rather take in a movie and just pick me up after the affair. This hurt me beyond words but I did not want to insist because I knew it would only hurt his feelings. Most of the time I was brought home by one of the faculty from the Institute of Arts.

Ping did not mind at all how late I came home. He was usually cheerful and he even asked me how I had enjoyed the party. Strangely too, he was not as eager to make love as he used to when we were both awake at that late time. He did not even care to come to my bed. I was hurt, but I kept quiet. Could it be that his job of having to work with numbers and accounts was killing his usual sex urge?

Then one Sunday when I was keeping the room tidy, he came and suddenly pulled me down to his bed and asked:

"Aren't you surprised you haven't been pregnant for more than six years now?"

"Well, I can't be pregnant all by myself," I answered in a sour mood.

"Oh, but I thought you were avoiding any love tangle with me because it might detract from the popularity you are now enjoying." And so we made love. For some reason, I wasn't really satisfied. It was like a piece of dried bread thrown to a hungry beggar. But I did not complain. After all, there was the dictum that a wife should never refuse her husband the pleasure that he sought, and I believed that by complying, I was doing my duty as a good wife.

When I was rehearsing the full length play *Call Me Mike,* I was always coming home late because I really wanted to make the actors live their roles. Once or twice I came home past midnight on a Friday. My classes on Saturday started at 10:30 so I did not have to get up so early.

"Who brought you home?" Ping would ask.

"Oh, as usual Joe Santos," I said. (To respect his privacy, I am not using his real name here).

"Was anyone else with you?" Ping asked.

"Mila who plays the role of the maid. She lives in Tanduay Street. Why?"

"I don't think it is healthy for you to be seen alone with him so late at night. People will think there's something fishy between the two of you."

"But he is not the only man they see bringing me home," I said quite casually. "Whenever you refused to escort me to a party or any school affair one of them always had to take me home. You're not suggesting people would think I could have an affair with all of them, are you?"

"Lately, I've noticed that it is always he," Ping remarked.

"Come on, Ping. That's because he's the one helping me with the play."

"You can't always be sure of how he feels for you, can you? I'm just trying to tell you not to be alone with him too much,"

"You can't be jealous! Ping, you're actually acting jealous! Don't tell me now that you are. Everybody knows I'm married to you and they also know you."

After that big show, we presented several small one-act plays on makeshift stages with very little scenery. I emphasized training in the interpretation of a role. So I gave exercises in the development of the actor's tools. My theater-lover friend was always there in constant attendance, sometimes conducting breathing exercises while I supervised the eurhythmic exercises. He must have wondered how a married woman with three children could lose herself so completely in her school duties as I did. One day, when we were having a breather, he asked me, "And how does your husband take all these frenzied activities of yours?"

"He doesn't seem to mind," I remarked very quietly. "Anyway he has his own activities as well." And he looked at me with a quizzical eye.

"Oh you poor suffering angel," he said putting his hand on my shoulder and letting it rest there.

"Please don't ever say or do that again or I will never allow you to help me." I said.

"Sorry, I promise I won't. But if there is anything I can do, please let me know."

"I will...and thanks," I said.

One night, I came home at about eleven o'clock. Ping was not home yet. I thought maybe their office at the Manila Port Terminal had a special visitor and all the employees had to attend the dinner. So I showered, got into my pajamas and went to bed.

Soon he came home and after parking the car in the garage, he came up by the kitchen stairway and started banging at the door. He never came in that way before. He had a key to the main door but this stairway was closer to our room. As soon as he came in, he undressed himself throwing his clothes any which way. Then he looked at me.

"What are you doing?" I asked, looking at him surprised. He never did that before, and was usually neat about folding his clothes or putting them either in the laundry basket or hanging them up.

"Take your clothes off, come to my bed. I want you," he said. His words were slurred.

"What?" He had never been harsh nor commanding before and I was caught off guard. Before I could say anything more he pushed me on the bed and was immediately on top of me." I was outraged and thought to myself, "This is rape. This must be what it is like to be forced." But I humored him because I realized he was drunk. I was just an accessory to his sexual urges. I was terribly hurt—physically and morally—but still, I did not complain.

The next day I had to call in sick and asked that a substitute be found to take over my classes. I could hardly walk. I was aching, literally and figuratively. I was a fool for thinking that since his job dealt mainly with numbers, he would be a serious husband and start spending more time considering his family.

That morning, Ping woke up with a hangover. He came to me full of apology over the way he had behaved the night before and started to explain. He said that his boss, Don Enrique Razon had a bachelor's party for one of the staff who was getting married and invited some first class call girls to liven up the occasion.

"Ping, do you find our relationship a drab routine?" I interrupted.

"No, no sweetheart, you could never be drab. We always enjoy ourselves together, don't we?"

"Okay now tell me more about those 'call girls'. Are they after money? Or excitement, or experience?"

"These were all well-educated, pretty and clean girls in their late teens or early twenties who have been trained to give unusual pleasure to men who can afford their rates. They mingle with the elite in high social circles and only those who have had some experience with them would know about their other personality. They have different names as call girls. One can call them through special telephone numbers for groups or singly. And they all have their tricks to avoid pregnancy."

But deep inside me I was happy because he was beginning to feel insecure about me. Every night after we had that exchange, he would wait for me and always greeted me eagerly. Often, as I was getting undressed, he would stop me and do it for me and we would make love. And I was always so ready, so willing and so able.

"Wow, that really impresses me," I said sarcastically. "And how different are they from whores, if you will permit me to use the word?"

"They do not stand in street corners, nor are they gaudily dressed. And they do not whisper in a bedroom voice 'How about a quickie with a terrific climax?'

"Oh, do they do that?" I asked him. "Are you telling me then that call girls are nothing else but first class whores?"

"You may call them that if you wish...but let's not talk about them, please, honey?"

"Okay, one last question. Why did you not go for the first class service the night you got drunk? Why did you have to pick on me?"

"I did! All of us did. It was free and we were expected to enjoy it. But Babe, Sweetheart I did not enjoy it at all. So I came home in a huff."

"So you came home in a huff, and I got raped!" It must have been the way I said it but for some reason, it sounded funny, and we both laughed.

## Chapter Eleven

"Before I forget...your father called," Ping told me.
"What about?"
"He said that we should take Tony out of San Beda."
"Why? It's so convenient to have him go there?" I was a bit peeved by this.
"That might be so, but Tony is hearing too many bad words in Spanish and he uses them without even understanding what they mean."
"My heavens! Have you heard him say them? Where has he gotten this?" I wondered aloud.
"From the hundreds of *mestizos* whose parents are not too careful with their language when their children are around. Don't blame the young ones. They don't always know they shouldn't use those words." Ping was amused that I acted surprised. "What word, for example?" I asked.
"Why? Do you want to use them too?" Ping teased.
It was then I realized that San Beda was really full of the sons of old Filipino-Spanish families who spoke what the late senator Recto called "*Español de la calle*"*. I had always known Spanish to be a very beautiful, romantic language but I also realized it had vulgar terms, just like any other language. So Tony was immediately transferred to the Ateneo de Manila in Intramuros, the magnificent Walled City of old Manila. His grandfather brought him to school in the morning and Carlos the driver picked him up in the afternoon. But we did have him during the weekends.
Life was pleasant and normal during that time, Ping with his cashier's job which he seemed to enjoy immensely, and me with my full time teaching at FEU. I saw to it that we had a drama presentation during each semester, and a debate between the two debating clubs.

*\*Street Spanish*

At home *Tía* Naty enjoyed her job of supervising the life of the two girls, and she was a strict disciplinarian. They did their homework after school, then had a little free time for some games before they took their afternoon shower. After that they got their clothes ready and school things for the next day, then had their dinner and after some quiet time, they were ready for bed. My brother-in-law, Onching, would come around once in a while and tell them stories which he invented for them on the spot. What amused the children was that he would even act them out. It was no wonder they loved having him around.

One night when I was brought home by one of my co-professors, Pepe Africa, Ping also arrived at about the same time. Ping got out of his car and met us.

"Thanks a lot for bringing my wife home, Pepe. I hope you brought her home still in one piece." he teased.

"You're welcome," Pepe answered, "But why don't you check it out yourself. After all, all I did was bring her home." and they both laughed. I caught the double meanings and I was not pleased.

It was almost Thanksgiving and our two plays for the Christmas program were not quite ready. Our rehearsals became longer and oftener, which meant that I got home later. This time Ping showed his displeasure and asked whether all this was really necessary. I felt there was no need for me to answer.

**D**ecember 8 was the Feast of the Immaculate Conception and with it came the thundering news of the Japanese attack on Pearl Harbor. The radio receivers of every house in the neighborhood were blaring that the United States had Declared war on Japan after its treacherous attack on Pearl Harbor. At the same time as this was going on, church bells were ringing, calling the faithful to the early Mass celebrating the Feast of the Immaculate Conception.

I wanted to assure myself that news of the war was only a nightmare, that soon I would wake up and continue living peacefully with my family. But no! It was all so real. We were all awake—Ping preparing to go to work, my two girls getting dressed for school.

"Let's just stay calm and wait for instructions. I'm sure we will be told something at work," Ping said. And so we carried on. Ping went to the office as I did, but I told the girls that they were not to go to school that day.

As Ping had said, at the FEU, the big sign at the gate said in big letters that all faculty members were to convene immediately in the auditorium. President Nicanor Reyes Sr. was already at the podium, facing the anxious faces around him, was trying to make himself heard above the noise. When everyone quieted down, he announced that all classes and activities of the school were suspended until further notice. We were to proceed to the Accounting Department where each of us would be given one month's salary. Two weeks after that, we would receive half a month's pay each, and that was it. FEU could not afford to assume commitments after that. He wished us all good luck and we all left, feeling anxious and sad. Fate had forced something on all of us unexpectedly and we didn't know how to deal with it. While we were all aware that the war raging in Europe could spread to Asia, none of us thought it would come this close and so soon. But here it was and in a wink of an eye, our lives were put on hold, dazed and not knowing what would come next.

With our ears tuned in to the radio once more, we learned that all schools and offices were immediately closed and further information would be announced over the radio. The radio warned that we could also expect an air-raid anytime considering our proximity to Japan and our being a Commonwealth under the United States. Sure enough, around noon of that day, the news was all over the place that a squadron of Japanese planes, all of them proudly displaying the emblem of the rising sun, flew overhead in perfect formation and dropped bombs somewhere near Intramuros.

"My God!" I screamed. "That's where the Ateneo is!" I worried about Tony and rushed to the telephone. Fortunately, I got to the Headmaster of the Grade school who assured me that the boys were all safe in the gymnasium and very little harm was done in the area. Almost at the same time, my father, who was in the offices of the Department of Finance called to tell me he was picking Tony up. This was our first taste of the reality that we were now a part of the war.

Ping who was chief cashier of the Manila Port Terminal was in his office at the Manila Port Terminal distributing money to the employees who would have to be laid off because of the war. He also said his job would have to continue until further notice because there would be many ships coming into the city. To reassure him, I told him Papa was picking Tony up right away and he needn't worry.

The next day, the Japanese planes came again but this time their target was the US Army installations at Nichols Field in Pasay City. Suddenly, I remembered that my mother-in-law's house was in that area. In the event that any of the bombs missed their target, she would surely get sick with fright and anxiety.

"Let's get them to live with us here until this is all over," I called Ping, and without wasting any more time, I called Mama Omeng up and told her and the family to start packing because Ping would pick them up after he finished what he was doing at the office. Then I called Ping and told him to pick up Mama and her brood as soon as he could. It might take two or three trips in the car but we had to do it then.

As soon as my father found out that I had asked my in-laws to stay with me, he called the farm manager who sent us via the truck that brought other supplies every week, six sacks of rice, a sack of refined sugar and a huge crate of vegetables. My mother called to tell me to buy lots of dried fish, beans and other non-perishables that could be stored without a refrigerator.

Fortunately, we had two living quarters in the spacious house. The tenants occupying the first floor had promptly vacated the apartment to return to their own homes as soon as they heard the war had come. I felt that my mother-in-law and her family of nine would be comfortable living there.

The saddest part about those days was when we had to take my brother-in-law Freddie, younger than Ping, who was called for active duty. We had to go to Tagaytay where he had to enlist. Seeing him go, my mother-in-law started crying and, pretty soon, so did I. We did not know if we would ever see him again. As it turned out after the Fall of Bataan, we received the news that he was "missing in action"

*In* 1942 when the Japanese Forces marched into town, Dr. Reyes called me up saying he was sending me some money that I might need for the duration. He also gave me some tips about how to conduct ourselves should the Japanese come to our house. Because Ping was fluent in Japanese, a language he had learned from his travels he was asked to remain as cashier at the Manila Port Terminal. The first thing that the Japanese soldiers did was to commandeer all the available cars in the locality. People had to walk or ride a bicycle. That was where my biking prowess came in handy.

There had been several instances mentioned of Japanese soldiers slapping people because they could not understand one another. So I told Ping I wanted to study Japanese and be ready to explain a situation should a problem arise. He approved immediately and I enrolled at the Nakashima San Japanese School where Ping was my tutor. Several Philippine government officials were there too. We met three days a week and I really enjoyed the lessons although the language was a world different from the English or Spanish or French that I already knew. After six months of study and a little practice Nakashima San announced that I was the valedictorian and that I had been selected to deliver the valedictory speech in Japanese at the closing ceremony.

My brother-in-law, Enrique whom we called Titong or Ike, and several of his friends from FEU decided to join the underground movement or "guerillas" who reported to Gen. Carlos Romulo, then already in hiding in a mountain in Luzon. When Gen Romulo heard that I was to speak as the valedictorian of the class he sent me a note: "Under no circumstance must you speak at that program. The US is watching all activities there. Do everything you can to avoid it." So two days before the program I was "sick with a bad throat" duly certified by Dr. Jose Fores, the only doctor the Japanese believed because he had lived in Tokyo for some time.

Money was starting to get scarce and I needed to do something for an income. Ping's salary could barely take care of all our needs. From a relative of mine I heard that the best income generating source would be to "buy and sell." People who had lost their jobs and their livelihood would try and get what they needed by selling their valuables. At that time all the banks had been sealed by the Japanese and no one knew how long they would remain that way.

My father left us a big amount of cash that he had collected from the Canlubang Sugar Estate for the sugar they had sold there but that too might not last too long, depending on when the war would be over. *Papá* decided to go back to the province with my mother, sister and her husband. He wanted to take all of us along, but I told him that Ping still had his job and since he spoke fluent Japanese and was able to get along with his Japanese employers, I felt we would be all right. I persuaded him to leave Tony with us and he agreed. That was the first time I felt that my son was really mine.

So that was what I did—buy and sell. Many who had priceless heirlooms they had been keeping for years were selling those to avoid going hungry. On the other hand, many people who suddenly became rich by working with the Japanese wanted to buy valuables for posterity.

To help with transportation shortages, Ping bought a *carretela,* the horse-drawn vehicle that was a familiar sight when I was still growing up. It was used to carry small cargo or five to six passengers. By that time, there was no more fuel for whatever was available had already been confiscated for the use of the Japanese army. Ping also bought a mare from a friend and I called it Rosalie. When people asked why, I told them the name just popped out of my head and besides it gave class to what was otherwise a common situation. It was Titong who drove the vehicle which often earned enough for us to buy a few important things for the house like soap, besides paying for the horse feed.

My other source of income was the "mahjong party". When the children were still small, my mother had a playhouse constructed at the very end of the backyard where they and their friends could play. This was to save their bedrooms and parts of the main house from being ruined by some of their very active games. The house held all their toys and they could play as noisily and roughly as they wanted to without disturbing their elders. When I decided to start my mahjong party, I thought this would be the best place to do it since it was large enough to accommodate five mahjong tables and their players and a few kibitzers too. Once or twice a month, I organized a "mahjong party" where I collected some *tong* enough for the family food budget of one or two weeks. For those unfamiliar with mahjong, *tong* is 10% of every winner's take dropped in the box for the refreshments served.

My father also sent some cash from the collection of the produce and other farm products that the trucks were allowed to take to Manila for the few hotels owned by Filipinos. Although I told my father not to worry about us because we were okay, I suppose he could not desist from helping, something that he had been doing all my life. This way, we survived the Japanese occupation without too much hardship.

*I*n 1942 a group of Ateneo alumni and some girls from the Assumption College formed a drama group called the Dramatic Philippines, an association which was allowed to present only Tagalog or Spanish plays. English was completely taboo in those days. My son, Tony, and I joined the group to escape boredom. We had a very good translator to Tagalog in the person of Francisco Soc Rodrigo, who much later in his life became a senator.

Our first big presentation was *Ang Martir sa Golgotha* a translation of the Passion of Christ written by one of the Jesuit priests. It was shown during Lent at the great Metropolitan Theatre on Plaza Lawton which was designed by Jose Arellano. Tony, who was then 13 years old, was in the cast playing the dead boy that was resurrected by Christ. I believe it was Emma Benitez Valeriano who played one of the women who accompanied the Blessed Mother played by Elvira Ledesma Manahan. Directing the play was Narciso Pimentel whom we called PIM for short.

We put on several plays that season. One of them was *Tía Upeng*, a translation of *Charlie's Aunt*, in which I played the lead role of the real aunt. At other times I did the costumes or took care of the props or was the stage manager.

The Japanese Forces assigned a captain who supervised our rehearsals and to see to it that it was not a front for subversive ideas. We soon discovered that Captain Yokamo was a graduate of Harvard University and spoke very good English.

*I*n 1943 we had a special event in our family. One morning Titong came to me and said he wanted to get married. One of the students rehearsing for our Christmas play when the war broke out was his chosen fiancee. Ping was fiercely against it. He said we should wait until the war was over. But I was sorry for poor Titong who was pleading with me to convince his brother to agree.

"All right!" I said, "You shall be married."

Ping warned me that it was not the right time for a wedding. "You shall be solely responsible for that if anything goes wrong," Ping warned me.

"Of course," I said very confidently.

When Ping was in the office the next day I went to my mother-in-law and asked her to help me. If she could call the relatives in San Pedro Makati to cooperate we could do it. I told her I had some money saved from my teacher's pay and we could spend that. I would also ask *Papá* to help.

So my father took charge of the Quiapo Church expenses, I took care of the brides's needs—wedding gown, ring, and small attendants— *Tío* Inong was the chief cook assisted by his family, and *Tía* Nena was to decorate the playhouse and backyard where the reception was to be held. My mother took care of the flowers. I made the wedding gown out of materials that I got on my father's account from the fabric store of his very good friend Mr. L. Aguinaldo. I bought a couple of rings from a pawnshop near our school. The vehicle that was to be used by the bride and groom was a decorated *calesa* with a driver dressed for the occasion. All in all, it was a cheerful and happy event. After some months we had a pretty little baby girl in our midst who was baptized Teresa.

In 1944 we were told that the house might be taken over by the Japanese Army because they needed to concentrate five units in one area. We believed they were preparing for a possible battle to defend Malacañang if the US Army came with General MacArthur. The one who brought us the news was a Japanese in the Occupation Forces was our Harvard-educated friend, who was also a friend of Titong's. My mother-in-law was worried. "Where can we go?" she wondered. I told her not to worry because the house in San Juan was empty, my parents having moved to the province with my sister and her family.

Ping, however, asked his Japanese friend in the office how true the news was and he was told that the Japanese higher-ups had changed their minds. They would place the units closer to the Sto. Tomas area where the American prisoners of war were kept.

Considering the uncertain moves of the Japanese Army which happened all too often, I was very worried about my piano. It was an old German Winkelmann that held all of the beautiful memories of my childhood. I saw what they did to my friend's piano when they took over her house. They chipped it to pieces and used the wood for fuel. It pained me to think of anyone doing it to my piano. So I sold it to someone who lived in Batangas and I cried for two days after it was gone.

In the latter part of 1944, Nakashima San, my former teacher in Japanese, asked if I could teach English to some officers and soldiers at Fort Santiago whose job it was to interview prisoners. In those days a refusal to do something always brought suspicions of subversive inclinations so I said I would try but I did not have the command of the Japanese language and it might be a bit difficult. In Fort Santiago where the Japanese jailed all those the suspected or found plotting against the government one, had to be very careful with one's language. I found out that three Japanese officers there were graduates of Yale University with Bachelor degrees in Political Science. One of them sat in the class that I taught. That's when they found out that I spoke and wrote Spanish correctly. Because of this, they offered me a good promotion as translator. I was to translate the message that Spain delivered everyday. Spain was Japan's ally then. When Carlos P. Romulo heard this from my brother-in-law again, he said "NEVER." His reason was that if the Japanese should retreat when the US Army returned, they would never leave me alive. Again, Dr. Fores told them I had tuberculosis, a disease the Japanese very much feared. So I was readily fired.

Sometime in 1943 all radio receivers were ordered to be thrown away because of their short-wave capacity. Anyone caught with a shortwave receiver was put to death. But I had a tiny set which I kept hidden in a pile of firewood in the garage. Sometimes, at midnight, I listened to the state of the war in the light of a votive candle. I knew that if the Japanese ever discovered me I would lose my head, literally.

The saddest thing I remember about this time was when Meneling came to tell us that his wife, Julita, was missing. She had gone to a place where casino games were played and which the Japanese suspected was a front for subversive activities. We all prayed very hard but she was never found. It was Meneling who convinced us to convert the playhouse and backyard into an air-raid center. "When the US Army comes to liberate us, the Japanese will not offer us to their enemy on a silver platter," said Meneling. "You are in the area near Malacañang which puts you in the war zone." So he brought some thick canvas and lots of sandbags and iron frames. In less than a week, we had a safe air-raid shelter that could house all of us.

Our English speaking Harvard graduate Japanese friend brought me a radio set one day. "Keep it until you have need of it," was all he said to me. After a while, he said, "Try to avoid going to the other side of the river to play Jai Alai. You are just throwing your money away." When I laughed he said, "Really, take me seriously. It may be demolished any time without any announcement so if you are caught on the other side when they do that, what will you do, then?" It may have been said in jest but I did not take it that way because I sensed he was serious.

That made me suspect that the Japanese Army was preparing to retreat. So I went to my own short wave radio that night and listened. Indeed the US Army was already somewhere in Luzon on its way to

Manila. I told only Ping about it so he started fixing up the shelter when most of the people were somewhere else so they wouldn't notice. Then he started stocking it with essentials.

One day some weeks after that, as I was walking in the street to go to play mahjong at a neighbor's house, a man riding a bicycle came near me and said in Tagalog, "*Dumating na ang ating mga kamaganak. Umui na kayo at huag kayong magpapapasok ng sinoman.*"* He did not know we had an air-raid shelter.

I aasked Ping to bring down the image of the Sacred Heart of Jesus and place it in the shelter. Then I told *Tía* Naty to take the girls to the shelter and bring some toys and books to keep them busy. Salvacion, our maid, took our wood burning stove to its designated place in the shelter as we knew that the gas would be cut off soon.

Ping remembered the baby. Where was the little girl? She was with some Japaneser officers who were playing with her. Tony and Titong went to get her. The Japanese wanted to come to the house with them but Titong said there was somebody who was sick in the house and they might catch the infection. So they did not insist.

When I went up to check if all the windows were closed I saw a tank in front of the San Beda College with the big US star on it. My heart skipped a beat. The US Army had really come. In less than an hour ten or more trucks went rolling in to Malacañang, shooting as they went after the Japanese in their military quarters.

We were all huddled together in the shelter praying the Rosary after eating lots of rice, scrambled eggs and fried salted fish. We did not know how long we would be stuck in the shelter. I gratefully thought of Meneling for the idea of the shelter!

The battle for Malacañang continued through the night. Several times over we would hear a truckload of Japanese soldiers shouting "Banzai" towards the Palace followed by the "rat-tat-tat" of machine

---

*"*Our relatives have arrived. Go home and do not let anyone into your home."*

guns and then silence.

In the moorning everything was quiet, but the streets and the corners were littered with dead Japanese soldiers.

Dr. Basilio Valdez and his brother-in-law, Dr. Legarda, who lived in the neighborhood went around asking the men to help bring the corpses into the vacant building between our house and theirs. It took them two or three hours to do that. Then they poured some gasoline on them and set them on fire. Otherwise we would not have been able to live with the stench of putrefying human flesh. As the bodies burned we also had to wear masks for the smell was intolerable.

Ping remembered an old American family who were held prisoners during the war at the Sto. Tomas Hospital. Dr. Fanton, a dental surgeon, and his wife and two children had been there for more than three years. He decided to go and see how they had fared. I told Ping I wanted to go with him even if only to see how the other streets were. But my mother-in-law said no woman should be going around under such conditions. But I said I would not be dressed as a girl. I put on a pair of gray pants, and a long-sleeved blue shirt and kept my hair inside a baseball cap and I really looked like a boy.

All the streets were littered with corpses and army trucks were picking them up like chopped off branches of trees and putting them in an open truck. Suddenly there was a jeep with American soldiers shouting, "Duck! Snipers!" Some people in a jeep were shooting everywhere. Ping pushed me and Tony ducked right away. But I lost my balance and fell across a dead Japanese soldier. As soon as I smelled it I jumped up saying "I'd rather be shot at than be on top of that."

Attempts at reconstruction were rather slow in this the northern part of Manila. The streets were cleared of all corpses in three or four days after the liberation of Malacañang. But in the south, the fighting was still going on. The Japanese chose to make that their last line of defense. Many were massacred in their own homes and unfortunately,

Dr. Nicanoor Reyes was one the victims together with his wife and three children. US Army trucks and jeeps took the fleeing wounded to the Nagtahan Bridge near Malacañang so they could be taken to a hospital.

Meneling called to tell me that his brother Irineo, the dental surgeon and his wife were among those crossing the bridge. Their home had been taken over by the Japanese. So Ping, Titong and Tony went to Nagtahan to watch and wait for them. And sure enough Irining and his wife Carmen, looking very ragged and tired, having run so much, arrived carrying a small bag of clothes and essentials. We gave them the girls' room and Tony went down to the bachelor's quarters after giving up his room to his sisters.

As the city groped slowly to a state of normalcy the courts were already trying many cases of people who had cooperated with the Japanese during the Occupation and were giving them due sentences. I kept saying a prayer of thanks to Carlos P. Romulo who had warned me about any appearance of cooperation.

My problem was what to do in the meantime since schools had not yet reopened. True, there was so much to do at home, but *Tía* Naty and my mother-in-law could very well take care of that.

My parents and my sister's family were back from the provinces and were already living in San Juan.

Then one day I got a call from the office of Captain Charles Vance who was in charge of Special Services in the US Army. He said that I had been highly recommended by several members of the faculty of the Far Eastern University to head a group of entertainers that would go to cheer the men in camps all over the Philippines. Of course I was interested. I saw him at his office at the Rival Memorial Coliseum. I was to head the biggest of five groups that would go around entertaining the men who had been fighting non-stop for 20 months. It would be called Filipiniana and would be composed of at least 45 people consisting of 15 dancers, 15 singers, six members of the *rondalla*, the string band that would furnish the music, a dance directress, a musical director, an emcee and a production crew of six. At first I was overwhelmed by the size of the group. I was only 37 years old, and every group I handled had always carried the support of FEU.

"But" Captain Vance said, "Here you have the backing and support of the US Army."

Quite true. Besides, after working to earn some lousy "mickey mouse" money I would be paid seven hundred dollars a month plus overtime in US dollars. On top of that, I would have other privileges. I would have a car and driver for my needs and the pay would start as soon as we began rehearsing.

I started burning the telephone wires immediately. Mrs. Francisca Reyes-Tolentino who was the head of the UP Physical Education for women and taught folk dances, was my choice for the Dance Directress and she was the one who would choose the dancers both male and female. Mr. Francisco Buencamino, my piano teacher in childhood, was my Musical Director. He selected the musicians.

And this is where all of us learned about US Army discipline. Two Army officers were assigned to train our group, Lts. Jim Sweeny and John Smith.

"When the director says 'Places!' you have five minutes to do that. I don't care if you are in your bras and panties, you have to be at your places because the curtain will rise after that in five minutes. Failure to be ready may bring a fine."

This was also the time when I met many Hollywood celebrities like Bob Hope, Lew Ayres, Joe E. Brown, and the Broadway director, Elijah Kazan. The stage discipline I acquired during this time, I later put into practice in training the FEU Drama Guild.

Ping was very supportive of me because it was a very challenging job and most of all because it brought almost three times what he was earning in Philippine pesos. But when he found out that Jose Santos, who helped me in all my drama projects at FEU was the coordinator of all the groups, he showed his displeasure. Frankly, I did not know that Jose Santos would be around until I found him at one of our rehearsals taking down notes on the progress of our show. He said that the same people who recommended me were the ones who gave his name to Captain Vance.

There were many things that I learned from the US Army. First and foremost was the strict enforcement of punctuality. I learned not to give any one more than five minutes grace. Later on, it was this practice in particular that made my students call me "the terror" of FEU.

I also learned to go up and down a plane using the perpendicular ladder instead of the comfortably inclined steps that commercial and official passengers used. At the beginning we wore the brown skirts of Army women, but these skirts would get blown up when we got down those perpendicular steps revealing everything we had underneath. So I passed a memo making all the women wear regulation brown pants.

Another thing we learned was to live—and not just sleep—in tents when the hot afternoon sun was shining on them as we tried to get rested for the evening show. There were always two armed guards patrolling our tents lest some men lose their minds and do some dastardly act seeing the women sleeping in their bras.

Before we left for our first show in Pangasinan, Captain Vance gave us a talk saying that most of the men who would be watching our show had not seen a woman in twenty months. So, if there should be any untoward incident or misconduct by any of them a report should be made immediately to the officer-in-charge at every station. Fortunately no such incidents of this nature happened during the existence of the group.

Another thing which I learned which I cannot say was any good was my smoking. Every Friday boxes of cigarettes of different brands were distributed to the officers in the office but they always skipped my table because I did not smoke. So, Lt. Sweeny took it upon himself to teach me so I would not feel left out. Ping was strongly against it as he did not smoke himself, so I never smoked at home.

It was also at that time that I became acquainted with the condom. These days it is so freely talked about that even grade school children know about its existence and use. The fact was that Ping had never used it with me, something Lt. Sweeny could not believe. Every Friday small things wrapped in multicolored foil which I thought was chocolate candy, would be distributed, but my table was always skipped. So I complained to the officer beside me saying there was discrimination in the Army. When I explained the situation to him he laughed loud and long.

"What's so funny?" I asked.

"Those, young lady, are condoms for the men.

"And what's that?" I asked.

"You mean you do not know what a condom is?" he asked in utter disbelief.

"And why should I?" I asked still surprised.

"I will tell you later," he promised as Captain Vance called him for a conference.

I really felt like a hopeless idiot when he got me a sample and explained to me as scientifically as he could, its purpose and use.

Ping was between laughing and being annoyed at himself that I should get this information from a man other than himself. But I really felt like a super idiot learning about it only after I already had three children.

While Ping and I got along very well at that time, my wifely relationship with him was quite irregular and I really had no time to check on his activities since my schedule was never fixed and after each assignment, I had to write a complete report of the show and submit it to the office for the records. Oftentimes he would wait for me until I came home so we could enjoy making love and no matter how tired I was, I went through it because I loved him. Perhaps at times he may have noticed a lack of passion or desire on my part and the fact annoyed him because on occasion he would tease me about losing my "fire" and yet he could not do anything about it. He saw how tired I often was.

My father had warned me about hurting Ping's feelings especially when he learned of the presence of the one person who used to help me all the time with my shows. But I told him the group would not likely last much longer because in a few months the men would be called to active duty and the group would cease to exist. So we left it at that.

## Chapter Twelve

For about eleven months, the troupe went from camp to camp in the whole country, from the northernmost tip of Luzon to the southernmost province of Mindanao. Then, Captain Vance called me one day and said that the Navy wanted to "borrow" us because they did not have any entertainment groups. He said he had "lent" them smaller groups like Musical Interlude which had only eight people playing some classical music, and the Aires Filipinos, a group of ten playing and singing Spanish-inspired melodies. The Navy somehow heard about my group of dancers and singers and they wanted to see the show.

From the start, the group, especially the girls, was timid about this assignment because the men who were sent to contact us were unlike those from the Army with whom they were already familiar. These men were quite austere in their appearance and language. But, it was an assignment and so one day we boarded a small ship that took our company to Subic Bay, the largest US naval base in the area. I did not know what type of boat we were on nor was I familiar with the ocean that we had to cross to get to our destination. The unfortunate fact was that most of the girls were terribly seasick and even the men had queasy stomachs, so I had to cancel the show for that night.

Our quarters were more comfortable than those we usually were given in the Army camps and there was also an armed guard that watched us 24 hours each day. We were billeted in a new, beautiful quonset hut but were given the usual cots for beds. Two medical personnel from Sick Bay, which, I found out, was what their hospital was called, came to give the group some pills and medicine for their ailments. On top of that problem three of the girls suddenly and prematurely got their monthly periods, a fact the doctors said was due to the change of climate or the trip by boat. I found out there were no shops where we could buy the necessary pads for them. "They can make them at Sick Bay," one doctor said. I was sure that Sick Bay had never been that busy.

Two medical orderlies came to me asking for the specifications of the pads they were going to make for the first time during the war. At that time, there were still no women in the Navy, at least not at Subic Bay. After being given the size and all they needed to know they asked how many were needed. When they heard me say "At least six dozen" one of the orderlies shook his head.

I put in a report to Captain Vance the following day and told him about the sickness of the girls and the other problems that we had. He told me to ask for a plane immediately that would take us back to Manila.

When I informed the officer in charge of us about this, he said, "I guess you will have to talk to Admiral Kincaid about that."

So, just before the last show I went to see Admiral Kincaid to ask for a plane.

"Why do you need a plane?" he asked.

"Because the girls got sick on the boat coming over."

"God damn it! Those planes were not made to ferry show people around!" he cursed. I was taken aback by his sudden fit of temper, but before realizing it, I had shouted back at him.

"God damn yourself, Sir. Captain Vance said not to leave unless we were given a plane so I suggest you talk to him Sir."

He called an orderly and Capt. Vance was on the line. They talked for some minutes and then the admiral asked. "And where did you get this spit-fire of a manager you have here? Congratulations! Okay. I will send them back on a plane".

By the time our group was disbanded, schools were already allowed to open regular classes. I got my former full load and the job of coaching director of the FEU Drama Guild.

Ping was still at the Manila Port Terminal and was also very busy. He had been given a promotion and while it could have been a good thing, it did not help us. In fact, it only made our relations take a turn for the worse. His position meant there were more drinking sessions with the officers of his company at which the ubiquitous call girls were always in attendance. The loving we had both come to cherish during the war years was reduced to practically nothing since he would come home drunk and cross. He would speak in a very loud voice and berate me for every little thing he did not like about the house—the arrangement of the furniture, the food, the behavior of the children. Nothing seemed to be right. When he began to rant and rave, *Tía* Naty and I would just lead him to bed and let him sleep it out. That way, we could hope that the children would not have awakened and heard him.

When I asked him one day why he did not come to my bed anymore he answered brusquely "You don't need it! You must have already satisfied your need with your good friend who happens to always be at your beck and call."

It hurt to hear him say things like that. But I would also be angry. "You're crazy," I would say, and try to reason with him. "With eight subjects to teach and the Guild to coach and direct, I don't even have the time to sit for a moment."

Occasionally, he would realize that he had hurt me. At those times, he would apologize and come to me but by then our love-making had become perfunctory. This made me sad. I would remember what we once had and wish that somehow, I could bring back those days again.

Then one day *Tía* Nena told me that she had seen Ping in a restaurant with a very young woman of foreign nationality. They did not see her because she was just passing by and they were at a table near the door. That must have been the night he came home at midnight, drunk again and kicked the door open. I had given him a key to the back stairs, but he did not use it. I did not confront him with what *Tía* Nena told me, afraid that it would lead to another argument that would have awakened the entire neighborhood.

In the morning, however, when he did not have to go to work because it was a Saturday, I talked to him and told him there was no need for us to fight when one of two people who had sworn to love and cherish each other had fallen out of love. I said I knew he was going with a foreign woman and I was not upbraiding him for that. Once more, he protested that the woman was merely a passing fancy and that I should not pay any attention to gossip. She was one of the "refined" call girls whom he had befriended and he took her out once in a while

He did not drink for a week or so after that, but every time I came home he was waiting to accuse me of going to bed with Jose. I had known for sometime that he had become intensely jealous but I simply brushed it off, knowing there was no truth to what he believed. The fact was I had not even seen this man for some time because there was no play to prepare and he was a single man with a profession who went his own merry way.

What I disliked most was that he talked to the children about it telling them that I loved another man and to report to him whenever they saw him with me. I was trying to keep the children from knowing the state of affairs that their father and I were going through. Once, I even suggested that he pick me up from school so he could see exactly what I was doing there. The fact was he also had become jealous of my growing popularity as a good stage director in school and civic presentations.

I tried to make him realize that I was giving all my attention to him and the children and tried to please him in every way. Any time he approached me to make love I complied, even during those times when I was dead tired from work. If he wanted to eat out I would go with him even though I felt bad about wasting all the food there was in the house.

Then one night he came home very drunk again. I asked him if they had gone out with the call girls again, and he said he had been with only one of them that night but "this one knew so many tricks." He was so drunk that he was actually proud of what he had learned from the professional pleaser.

"What tricks?" I asked.

"Oh, here, let me show you. I'm sure you will love it!" He undressed quickly and told me to do the same.

"Come here, " he said. He was sitting down.

"What?" I asked

"Yes. Come, I will show you."

" Ping, you are drunk and I will not do this," I said. "The usual way is fine for me."

" It's like swimming. You love to swim, and you know there are many different strokes. Swimming only one way and using one stroke can be boring. Doing it different ways keeps it from getting monotonous," he said. "Come, I'm sure after you try it this way, you will like it!"

It might have been the mood I was in but I found it crude and disgusting and after all these years the episode still nauseates me. But at that time, I did what he asked me to the letter. I wanted to assure him that I was still his wife.

It was that incident, however, that reduced our relationship to the minimum. He began coming home later and later, claiming there were always so many things to do in the office, but I knew for a fact that it was not office work that was keep him away till past midnight. I made no complaints for the sake of the children, but I could not avoid the harsh words that we exchanged at times. I just prayed that things would change.

Then one night he came home a little earlier, wanting to make love. .the way I liked it, he said because he wanted to please me. For the first time in all the years we were married, I refused him. I told him that what I wanted was love, not charity, not a beggar's pickings. I said very clearly, that if he forced me, I would consider it rape. He left.

That night I wept, knowing that from hereon, our relationship could only go downhill. More than that, I realized that Ping and I had lost something that we once held very dear. I recalled the way we were such good friends during our courtship. We could talk about anything and everything. There was always laughter, and there was very much love. All that was now lost and I knew we could never get it back. I felt strongly that the way things were, we would probably never recover it. We had said and done so many things to each other that were painful and demeaning. We had hurt each other deeply, and were not ready to forgive. And I mourned the loss of all we had. When *Tia* Naty and the children asked why my eyes were red, I said something had irritated them. But I guessed that *Tia* Naty knew. Ping and I had lost the gift of showing our love for one another. Lately, there were only harsh words and I could see it in the faces of the children.

There were two people whom I went to see, telling them that I had come to the decision that it would be best for everyone that Ping and I live separately. These two were the only ones I felt I could trust: my father, and Father Reuter. Father Reuter told me that if that was how I felt, it would be best to leave, the sooner the better. I told my father everything and he asked me whether Ping had hurt me physically. I said no. Ping had never raised his hand to hit me. Papá advised that I talk with Ping about a separation in a civil manner and not ask for even one cent for support. Papá said he could still afford to educate all the children and support us. Proudly, I told my father that aside from the Ateneo which really was expensive, I could still take care of the two girls.

I cannot remember exactly how I was able to tell Ping that I had made the decision that since we seemed to have lost the love we once had for each other, rather than get the situation to become even worse, it would be better for us to try living apart. Perhaps being away from each other would help us think more kindly of one another. At any rate, this would be better than the constant shouting to which our communication had been reduced. If any change for the better would take place, then we could talk about it. He of course claimed that his love for me had not vanished, that it was still very much alive. But I had lost my faith and no longer trusted him. I also told him that it was he who had to go. I owned the house, and so it was he who had to leave.

I learned later that when he went home to his mother, he told her I had driven him out because I had a boy friend. Fortunately, she did not believe everything he said. I told her what had happened was that he was living with someone else and that when he came to me, he expected me to go to bed with him too. I told her that I could not accept that. Even though I was aware that this might have been the case in many households, I refused to be left with only pickings. Ping was my lawful husband. I was not about to accept only the pickings of a relationship.

On the day he left, Ping waited for the children to come home from school and told them about our separation. The children did not ask me any questions. Perhaps the change they saw taking place between their father and me was still beyond their understanding. Or perhaps, they were just happy that the quarrels and arguments between their father and me had come to an end. I did not want them to know how their father had started to treat me, so I told them nothing. The girls may not have been aware although I think Tony, always sensitive and observant knew that his father and I had lost something beautiful we once had.

One sad aspect about this whole affair was that I had not even been in touch with the object of Ping's jealousy for several months. Jose had his own business and profession to attend to and we saw each other only when I was faced with a direction problem in my theater activities.

But gossip always grows fast and the grapevine was full of our separation. It spread like wild fire in school, and among my friends. As the story went, Ping and I separated because I had a boy friend. In those times when a marriage went on the rocks, it was always the wife at fault. If she showed her jealousy over her husband's philandering, she was a virago that only drove him deeper into the arms of another woman. And if she should be seen being escorted by another man, then she was "loose" and had taken on a lover. The double standard had such a strong hold on Philippine society that no one saw it wrong for the man to "fool around" but a woman who was even remotely suspected of going out with a man other than her husband, was to be ostracized.

Father Reuter told me that I had started on my personal *via crucis* and he would pray to God to give me courage.

I did not know how to explain what was happening to the children. I tried to find the opportunity, but Ping got to them before I did. I did not have the courage to ask the children what he had told them, or perhaps, I did not want to know. I felt it best to keep quiet. I just prayed to God to help me so that my children and my parents would some day be proud of me. For months, I carried all these mixed feelings within me and to console myself, I threw myself into my work.

Blessed relief came about with my appointment as head of the FEU Radio Department. It was the lifesaver that brought me out of the dumps. I felt that I had been given a new lease in life.

*Chapter Thirteen*

As head of the FEU Radio Department, I was so busy that my Dean reduced my teaching load to three subjects all of which led to Radio Broadcasting, a significant "first" in Philippine Broadcast Courses in Asia.

My first step in the training for professional broadcasting was to write a long petition to the Department of Education asking that the courses then offered under a vocational curriculum be converted to legitimate college courses leading to a Bachelor of Arts in Radio Broadcasting. Fortunately the petition was approved.

In my faculty were well known radio personalities like Dick Taylor, Eddie Martelino, Justo Montemayor, Nick Agudo, Jose Reyes and Ruben Medina. Our program went for a half-hour on the air from Monday through Friday using the facilities of Station DZBB managed by Bob Stewart, a successful American GI of World War II. Teachers and students collaborated in writing scripts and rehearsing shows during the weekends. I taught subjects like Voice and Diction, Radio Drama and Microphone techniques.

The eighth floor of the Science Building was properly equipped and wired for broadcasting. We had a little stage for some live radio plays with invited guests. The offices and classrooms were on the seventh floor. I had delightful and humorous memories of our work there that helped me to exist in my newly chosen life as a single parent.

Mine was a terribly busy schedule—teaching and broadcasting, and at home seeing to the comfort of my children, who were very sympathetic towards their father and disappointed in their mother.

Unfortunately, this department of FEU was to last only a little over a year, for soon it was absorbed into the new and and more comprehensive Department of Mass Communications which added subjects on TV production, script writing. and more.

The traditional annual full-length play came all too soon. This responsibility rested on our shoulders. After a short meeting my group chose *Peg O' My Heart* as the characters in the play were more or less the same age as my students. As if from nowhere, my good friend, Jose showed up to help me with the production problems. He had heard about the break up of my marriage and promised to help me professionally and emotionally. We both laughed at this because I knew that we would be talking about the show and it would keep me from feeling lonely.

In reality, Jose and I liked many of the same things, and, we could talk about them endlessly for hours. He was not married and when we had to work longer than usual I did not have the problem of feeling guilty for unduly keeping him away from a wife or family.

One day when I was sketching the design for the scenery of our show I paused for quite some time looking at the trees outside my window.

"Five centavos for your thoughts." he said.

"They don't cost that much," I quipped.

"I bet you others have offered only one centavo, so I am offering four centavos more."

"I was just trying to remember if I had locked my desk drawer at home."

"Hidden treasures there? You want me to go and check?"

"No, not that important really. But thanks anyway."

"If there is anything." he said holding my hand, "anything at all—big or small—that you need help with, you can count on me."

Just like many others before you, I should have said. For a few acquaintances had surprisingly become very attentive to me after knowing I had broken off from my husband. They must have been thinking that a lonely woman would be easy prey for some illicit relationship.

One day he came all smiles to the rehearsal.

"What's making you so happy?" I asked.

"Do you know that the gossip is going around that you and I are having an affair?"

"Really?" I pretended to be surprised." And how do you feel about that?"

"Me? Of course I am flattered. I feel it is an honor to be spoken of in the same breath as you. Indeed I wish it were true."

"Most people cannot understand that a platonic friendship can and is possible."

And we continued working on the production, sometimes staying past midnight to polish some scenes. He picked me up for the rehearsals and brought me home after them and I was very grateful for all that trouble.

Then one rainy Friday night we finished rehearsals rather late. He suggested that we let all the actors and production staff go ahead and we would rest and wait until the rain had let up a bit. The rehearsal for the next day was in the afternoon and we could relax, he said.

Physically spent from the final coaching and directing I reclined in the sofa which was part of the furniture of the play. I must have fallen asleep for I was suddenly awakened by a sizzling passionate kiss on my lips. and a hand around my waist. Fired by a starving, natural human desire I wantonly agreed to end our platonic friendship.

At the rehearsal the next day I was very quiet. I was terribly confused by the sudden turn of events.

"What happened last night was terribly wrong," I told him.

"What is wrong in it? I have been keeping my feelings for you for a very long time. Quenching my burning desire to have you in my arms and aching to tell you what I feel. But I could no longer hold it back."

"That's not really right, " I countered.

"I want you to know that my intentions are honorable. I want to marry you."

"How can you do that? You know there is no divorce in this country."

"We can get married in Hongkong. And even live there. I can easily find a job. That would not be a problem. "

"You are forgetting that I have children. What do we do with them?"

"Oh we can support them. They are old enough to take care of themselves. Besides that, your husband is constantly poisoning their minds against you."

"No. Get this straight, I will never leave my children. I do not care what they think about me. They are my responsibilities before God and before man."

And our conversation ended there. We continued to work on the play which turned out to be a big success. And for a while things of the heart were put aside.

He came to see me in school whenever his work allowed him to do so, and I noticed that he was becoming very possessive of me, though he respected my social and professional obligations and patiently remained in the background.

My cousin Meneling who was very concerned about my separation called and took me out to dinner one evening. Jose also called asking me to go with him to dinner at a newly opened restaurant and I told him I had already agreed to go with Meneling. He suspected that it was with another friend who had been calling me up lately. So he parked his car a block away from my house where he could see me go out. I noticed his car but my cousin did not.

I told Meneling the whole truth and about the gossip going around.

"One thing I want you to tell me truthfully," said Meneling. Do you love him enough to spend the rest of your life with him?"

"No, no!" I cried, "He is very kind and helpful to me and we share many preferences about theater arts, but that's all. And what happened was due to a sudden human weakness. that overwhelmed me."

"Well, do not encourage him too much. Use every excuse you can think of not to be available to him. Pretty soon his desire will simmer down and he will look for some other activities."

"I will try to do that but at he moment he is dead set on owning me."

The next day I asked him why he was parked at the street corner to see who was picking me up.

"Because if it had been someone else and not your cousin there would have been a triple killing right then and there. I had my gun ready for that." And he showed me a small snub-nosed revolver.

"What a crazy idea. You cannot keep a relationship by means of fear. You have to generate love," I told him.

"But I cannot give away something that I have just begun to possess," he said.

I kept quiet but I had my own plans.

Meneling called to ask if I could take care of a show the Smiles Club was presenting at their anniversary affair at the Manila Hotel. It was not a play but a floor show of songs and dances with a theme, I readily accepted it because it would keep me from brooding over my painful loneliness. My unintended 'affair' did not really feel the void that I carried in my heart. Almost at the same time Miss Consuelo Francisco, executive secretary of the Philippine Mental Health Association called and aaked if I could find time to spend two hours every other Saturday to givie a session of "recreational therapy" to the recovering patients of the National Mental Hosspital. It was a voluntary service and no one qualified had accepted it.

"Sure!" I said "Anyway it would give me something to do instead of feeling miserable."

The Smiles Club was a select association of Manila's elite families. Aside from the celebration of Christmas, New Year and Easter, they always had an anniversary ball with a grandiose floor show. I was challenged and thrilled to do it. That kept me busy after my big show. Meneling picked me up for rehearsals and brought me home after them. So there was very little time for romance.

While friends and gossips talked about me and my "affair" I prayed every night asking God how I could free myself from a relationship that was not at all uplifting. Every Friday I went to the Quiapo church and lighted a votive candle asking the Black Nazarene to guide me in my difficult situation.

Because of all these commitments I had made, I could go out with Jose only two or three times a week, more often than not, for a movie and dinner as I needed to go home and finish some dresses my daughters would have to wear at a party or I had some house chores that demanded my attention. immediately.

Then Antonio Villegas, a former student of mine was elected Mayor of Manila. He appointed me Chairman of the Manila Film Festival that climaxed with the awarding of prizes very much like the Oscars of Hollywood. It was quite a job for I had to see twelve movies in two weeks. The Mayor gave me a pass and license plate that would allow me to park anywhere, even in prohibited areas to allow me to go to the theaters.

This put my name in various newspapers and radio newscasts again. According to my friend I was as popular as the Queen of England.

My increasing popularity got me invited to do some fund-raising shows for The Philippine Red Cross, the Philippine Anti-Tuberculosis Society, and the Philippine Mental Heaalth, all of which was volunteer work that was rewarded with a framed recognition of my efforts.

My father was very proud with the popularity I gained as a valuable fund-raiser, but he worried over the gossip about me.

"Don't worry," I said "I have faith that God will help me."

"On top of all my volunteer work for these civic and medical associations my good friend and cardiologist Dr. Alimurung asked me if I could put up some sort of fundraising show for the Feast Day of the Blessed Virgin of Bacoor, his home town in Pampanga. I owed him so many favors that I could not refuse him.

There was absolutely no time for romance and Jose could not do anything about it.

Very soon thereafter a One-Act-Play-Contest was announced by the Palanca Literary Awards, At stake was a big silver trophy donated by the US Embassy Dept. of Cultural Affairs. Six Schools registered for the Contest, one of then was Far Eastern University

My friend jumped at the idea. It meant working with me on a theatre project which surely would need his help.

But I stopped him short.

"Let me explain something," I began." I am very grateful for the help you have given me in all my past theater projects. In fact I have learned so much from you and I appreciate that too. But this is something different. It is a contest. If it should win I myself would not know how much honor I deserve and how much should you. I would like to do it alone this time. If it wins, the honor is all mine, and if it doesn't, well, I get the disappointment. I'm asking you to grant me this favor.

"But can I still pick you up and bring you home?" he asked.

"That is the favor I would like to ask you. My father is lending me his driver for the duration. His neighbor Mr. Leviste is giving him his car and driver as he will be in Batangas during those months. If my actors, the staff of production and the rest in the university always see you with me they will think that as usual you have a hand in the production."

He was silent for a very long while.

"If that is what you want, so be it. I can see that you do not care for me as much as I care for you."

"Thank you so much." I said. I did not mention anything about caring because I would be telling a lie.

I chose the English translation of Anton Chekov's *The Boor*, because there are only three characters and coaching would be much easier. In the title role was Frankie Evangelista, Victoria Oliveros, as the widow, and Butch Josue as the servant.

And we won!

According to some of my former colleagues who are still in Manila, there, the big silver trophy was still in the Department of Mass Commuication. My picture appeared together with my cast in all the big newspapers and my name was mentioned in all newscasts on the radio. Jose congratulated me half sarcastically, and my parents were proud of me though my mother was still unhappy about the gossip about me.

During my preparation of the play *The Boor* one of the teachers in my department told me that she had seen Jose more than twice with a young lady that many people said was his former girl friend. She asked if we were still seeing each other.

"Hardly," I said because I have been so busy with this play and we agreed that I would do it alone this time."

I should have been jealous at the news, but I was not. In fact I have been wondering how I could make him understand that we were not really cut out for each other as lovers. I am sorry that he was really in love with me so much, something I could not reciprocate no matter how much I tried. The news therefore made me feel that God was helping me somehow,

After the One Act Play Contest I noticed that he was no longer complaining about our infrequent times together. He was still very nice to me and I tried hard to return his attention, but he must have noticed I was exerting a lot of effort in doing so. I did not tell him about the news I had heard about him and his date.

About two weeks passed and he would call me but we could never go out because there was always something to do in the realm of my work. Even on the phone he was very sad and when I would ask him why he always answered that it was because he knew he was longing desperately for something he knew he would never have. I always tried to soothe him by saying that perhaps it was because God had something better reserved for him. And he would just sigh and hang up. Actually it broke my heart because I really felt sorry for him.

One day he called me at the office and said he had something terribly important to tell me and could I please say yes to dinner. I did and he picked me after class in the evening.

"Is anything wrong?" I asked when I saw him so sad.

"You know very well that you are the only one I have desired to be with for the rest of my life—I have asked you to marry me—not here because there is no divorce here—but in Hongkong. You flatly refused because of your kids. Day by day I have begun to realize that I cannot hope to have any future with you. You can see that it breaks my heart; but that is the way the chips fall.

I became very sad too, because he had been very close and useful to me in many ways. So I could not control my tears.

"I knew you were seeing your former girl friend and though I would hate to lose you, I have to agree that what you say is unfortunately true. You have the right to seek elsewhere what you cannot find in me. I am deeply saddened but we can still be friends and I will never forget the lovely times we've had together." It was not easy for me to say all that to him, but I knew I had to.

It was a very tearful goodbye and when we got home he held me very tight in his arms and kissed me hard. I was still in tears when

I got to my bedroom, but at the same time, I felt greatly relieved as if a big burden had been lifted from my soul.

Six months after that he was married at a beautiful ceremony and he and his bride honeymooned in Baguio. From there I got a wire on my desk that said. "I still wish you were here."

## Chapter Fourteen

Strange as it may seem I did not feel too bad about losing Jose. I still regarded him as a very dear friend, one whom I had counted on in times of need. He was always there to offer a ready hand when I needed one, and he was good company at those times when my loneliness would prevail over my better sense. But there never was any strong sexual attraction on my part. I never felt for him, the romance nor elation that accompanied the way I felt for Ping, even when things started to go wrong. It had not been easy for me to make Jose understand that. I felt that somehow I had shortchanged him because I could not match the deep love that he said he had for me and I should have told him this from the very start. So I was glad that he had made up his mind, and found what I could not give him. Nevertheless, I could not shake off the guilt I felt for having been so unkind and misleading him. I had thought only of myself and I felt bad. No one should ever toy with another person's feelings the way I did with Jose's.

As I was still feeling pretty disgusted with myself, the telephone rang and, looking back on it now, I continue to see it as a gift from above, one that I badly needed to shake me out of the mood I was in. The call was from Dave Harvey of the Manila Theatre Guild, a cosmopolitan group that regularly presented plays at the Army and Navy Club Theater. They needed someone who could direct a Spanish play. Dave asked me if I was willing to do it.

Immediately, I felt I had been given a new opportunity. What Dave was offering me was my cup of tea. No pay at all but lots of fun, and a chance to work with people who loved theater, who took it seriously, and who appreciated it. It might be hard work, but the results, I knew, would always be satisfying. Here was the beginning of my chosen career. And a mere telephone call got me on my way.

My first attempt was *Las Tres Perfectas Casadas (Three Perfect Wives)*. It played to packed houses for three weeks and by popular demand was extended to another week. I did not realize that there were so many people who were hungry for Spanish plays.

Then came the call from the Barangay Theatre Guild headed by Lamberto Avellana, the movie director. Daisy, Bert's wife had edited Nick Joaquin's play. *Portrait of the Artist as Filipino*, one I had refused to consider some years back because it was too long. It mirrored the typical life of the Filipino family during the change that took place as the values of the Spanish past were disappearing with the new ways of life that the American Occupation had brought with it. Barangay Theatre had decided to present the play and wanted very much to stage it, but had no money to spend..

"Don't worry," I said, quite confidently. "I will find a producer." I realized as I spoke that I had been too hasty in speaking since I did not even know where to begin.

First, we had to find a theatre we could afford, but Bert, as if reading my thoughts said, "I think we should present it *al fresco*. It would have a greater impact if we do it open air."

There was a vacant lot two blocks from the City Hall, quite close to the ruins of the magnificent Walled City called Intramuros. That seemed to be the perfect place to do it in the show in the dry season. So I went to see Mayor Arsenio Lacson, the Mayor of Manila, who thought it would be something different and readily gave us permission to do it there for as long and as often as we wanted to.

The next problem was the stage. Daisy and I went to the offices of the Santa Clara Lumber Company, a stockholder of FEU and had a part in the building of the FEU auditorium. The company promised to build a stage for us according to our specifications.

As for the lights I was not worried about them. Meneling had a shop called PHILIGHT, which had a good stock of spotlights for all occasions. His son, Tony, was assigned to help me with that. But, where and how would we get the electrical power? Again, Mayor Lacson came to our rescue and allowed us to connect with City Hall.

So one beautiful summer night, with the moon and a million stars lighting the sky as our backdrop, we opened to a full house.

In the cast was Daisy Avellana, playing the starring role of Candida, Dolly Benavides as her timid sister Paula, and the leading male character, Tony Javier played was played by Armando Goyena, (Ping Revilla in real life) the most loved movie idol at that time. Nick Agudo played the brother and I was Pepang, the bitchy older sister. Father Reuter, after the play, commented that I was a natural.

And so the years went by, gliding with time, and with work that I loved, and a lot of prayers, slowly the process of healing the deep wounds of the heart took place. I lost some friends who did not want to be seen with a popular civic and artistic personality who was, at the same time the focus of gossip. But these were fair-weather friends and the ones who stayed close, made up them.

Every time I came home, however, I was assailed by the memories of the one time happiness that Ping and I shared. The empty bed on one side of my room was a silent witness of the joy we once shared. And the pain of loss was as strong every time as the time he left. The living room sofa where I waited for him, the ordinary exchange of the things that made our day, the endearments, the hopeful anticipation of the love-making that would follow—all of these sharpened the feeling of tormenting loneliness.

It got to a point where coming home had become painful, so I called *Papá* to get his permission to sell the house. It had become too big for us. Having been sensitive to all my moods since I was a child, I knew he understood when he reluctantly agreed. We first moved to one of two apartments that my sister had built on my mother's garden. Then some months later, we moved to a small, pretty Swiss-style chalet on

N. Domingo Street with a spacious elevated garden and a terrace in front.

*I*n time my theater activities at FEU became bigger and better. In an attempt to relive the beautiful musical shows of the turn of the century, I decided to stage a *zarzuela* called *Ang Kiri* a name I had to change into *Ang Masayang Dalaga* because the FEU Catholic action thought that the word *kiri* applied to a woman of loose morals.

It was a difficult and expensive project but I wanted my students to develop a taste for the grandiose. I would not accept a less than 24-piece symphonic orchestra to accompany the operetta. In performances like this, the music can make or destroy the show. Fortunately the president and the Board of Trustees approved all my requirements. At that time FEU was the only school that attempted as big a show as this with students as actors.

In June of 1958 I was gifted with a miracle from God Perhaps this was a fitting reward for my volunteer services to the community and, at the same time, an assurance of God's love to assuage the pain of a solitary existence. This miracle was a beautiful baby boy who was given to me for adoption and he was a blessing that gave me a new purpose in life. Having been born on June 2, the Feast day of San Luis Gonzaga, just two days after the Feast of St. Joseph on June 19, he was baptized Jose Luis. When he was slightly ill with a cold or had gas pains, the whole family checked into the presidential suite of the FEU Hospital, for at that time I was concurrently executive secretary to President Nicanor Reyes Jr.

Time flew by so swiftly and my children got married one by one. First it was Tony who married the beauteous Concepcion Mendoza. Then there was Nenita to Roy Dahlen and Josefina, or Baby, to Fred de la Rosa.

Tony's reception was held at his best man Johnnie Taylor's house, while the two girls had theirs at our well-decorated elevated garden terrace. At Baby's wedding, Jose Luis, who was nicknamed Joey, was the ring bearer. Seeing the children all grown up and starting families of their own gave me a sense of accomplishment, but at the same time I also questioned myself whether I had done enough for them.

One day another phone call signaled that a change was about to take place in my life once more. My former French professor, Dr. Pura Santillam-Castrence who was then executive secretary at the Department of Awards at the US Embassy said I was recommended for that year's Fulbright scholarship by three persons: Carlos P. Romulo, Secretaary of Foreign Affairs, Father Reuter from the Ateneo University, and Dr. Vidal Tan, then President of FEU.

"Oh my god." I said." I don't think I can accept it."

"Why not?" she asked?

"Because my father is 84 years old and if anything should happen to him I am the only one who would know what to do. My mother and my sister have both passed away already."

"Oh what a pity," she seemed really sad that I had so quickly refused. "Well, come for the interview anyway. You won't lose anything. Besides we might be able to make possible necessary arrangements should your problem come about."

So I went for the interview. I was told that all the members of the committee were unanimous in their opinion that I should be given the scholarship. They gave me three weeks to make my up my mind.

It was a big step for me as I had never been abroad, and here the opportunity was mine to take or leave. I asked God to help me decide, and as most people who ask God to grant them something do, I asked Him to give me a red rose within one week if He meant for me to accept the scholarship. Any other color or flower would mean a "no". After three days, I had not received a red rose and so I resigned myself to having to give up the scholarship. On the other hand, neither had I received any other flower of another color.

The next day, as I was in my office listening to the recordings of my students in Voice and Diction, one of my Thai students whom we called Changko for short—Thai names being so long and hard to pronounce—came running into the room holding aloft a long-stemmed bright red rose and held it out to me. My heart leaped!

"Where did you get that rose?" I asked, finding nothing else to say.

"Near the Santa Mesa Church Ma'am. I got it for you because I know you love roses."

"Thank you, my Lord," I said choking in my tears.

"I'm sorry. Why are you crying, ma'am?"

"I am crying tears of joy, Changko. Thank you, thank you so much."

He looked rather perplexed.

On October 1, 1961, I was met at the Washington DC National Airport by Jackie Jardeleza, son-in-law of my first love at the UP. He was married to Lolita, the older daughter of Roming Ledesma.

The next day, Jackie took me to the Catholic University of America, Department of Speech and Drama, whose head was the unforgettable Fr. Gilbert P. Hartke. After getting enrolled, I was told to go to a graduate apartment building run by the CUA on 12$^{th}$ Street where I was to join three American graduate students. At that time all foreign students had to live with American roommates

I consider myself quite fortunate in getting my Fulbright Scholarship during the time of John F. Kennedy, the only Catholic president America has ever had. It was also a stroke of good luck that Fr. Hartke was the First Couple's spiritual adviser. A further lucky streak was that the President and his brother Robert, then Attorney General, had developed a liking for foreign students, considering them the "hope of the future." Thus, there were several occasions when we would meet them.

Our class in Acting was at 2:30 P.M. followed by one in Directing, both under Father Hartke. Several times during the semester Father would come about half an hour late because he had lunch at the White House, a fact he announced to the class with pride. He was always invited to the various concerts and other cultural and social activities that Mrs. Kennedy gave periodically and he had press passes to distribute to the media. Most of the time, Father Hartke would ask me to go to the White House for these events and I always went, even when it was snowing hard.

"You are not going to melt in the snow," he would growl at me.

That was how I got to meet several celebrities during that time, like the world renowned soprano and opera diva, Maria Callas—who was always escorted by her boy-friend Aristotle Onassis—the blind musician, José Feliciano, and many more.

The two Kennedy brothers frequently invited us to picnics or drove us to view the beautiful landscapes in the fall, or go to their big farm and learn to play touch football with the rest of the Kennedy family. There were times when the First Lady wanted to play but could not because she had her two little ones in tow. Sometimes, she would call me to mind Caroline and John John. Of the foreign students' group, I was he only one who knew some stories and songs in English because the other two were from Japan and Africa. It was having been in touch with Caroline and John John personally that made me weep when I heard of John John's accidental death.

The Department of Speech and Drama was quite full of events and performances. An old building at the entrance on Taylor Street where Drama classes were held and a makeshift theatre directly across were used for small plays that were regularly presented by the acting-directing class. For the big Shakespearean plays or on those occasions when a popular director or opera conductor were involved, the show was done at the Olney theatre in Olney Maryland.

I remember in particular dress rehearsal for a well known conductor's work, Igor Stravinsky's operetta *L'heure espagnol*. Together with another student, Bob Leighton, I was assigned to handle an outside spot mounted on a platform outside the stage near the orchestra section. At one point in the show, we were supposed to light the entrance of an important character. Stravinsky was a small man, just about five feet tall and he was very strict about cues. When our cue came, instead of focusing the spot on the actor I accidentally pushed it. My gloves were much too big for my hands, so the spot fell to the floor with a big crash. Somewhere from the darkness of the orchestra section I heard Father Hartke's thunderous voice, "DAMNATION!" followed by the very calm voice of Mr. Waring, our Lighting professor.

"It's okay. These things do happen. Richard!" he called for our gofer. As if this were a normal occurrence, he said, "Please go get another spot from the van."

Every year Helen Hayes came to CUA to star, for free, in a show designed to raise funds for the building of a new theatre on campus. When she came to Manila some years after my scholarship and we gave her a dinner at the Manila Hotel, she gave us the glorious news that Father Hartke had just received a donation of two million dollars for the Theatre. Then and there we promised to give our little donation of twelve thousand dollars as well.

With all the activities at the CUA, I still continued to stay in touch with the Filipinos both on and off campus. Sometime in 1962, I was called to a meeting of all Filipino students in CUA. I found out that the sweet little Filipino girl in the Library Department, Editha del Callar, was going to be married and since she did not have her family in the U.S., the association of Filipino Students would act as her family. The

Alzona Family offered their house for the reception, and Cesar Alzona, the husband, was going to give her away. Other wedding preparation assignments were given to different people present. One was to take care of the invitations; another, the church; another the food and still another, to arrange for flowers and so forth. When it came to me I didn't quite know what I could offer until I heard myself say: "I will make the wedding dress!"

"What? Are you serious?" This, from a chorus of voices.

"Yes I will do that."

I knew I could do this because of the experience I already had with my dress shop even though it was way in the past. The tricky problem was time. I had only three weeks to prepare. The following day I went to Woodward and Lothrop Department Store and got their Bridal book and chose the model I was going to make. When my roommates, Anne Ripon, Ann Clarke and Marlene Starke heard about it they offered to take over my household chores until the dress was finished. Well, it was done, and in good time, and the bride walked down the aisle, looking like an angel. I am sure that to this day, the dress still hangs in the closet of its owner.

When I returned to the FEU the first thing I did was to change the curriculum of the different courses in the Department of Mass Communications and adopt the one of the Catholic University. The UP immediately followed suit.

My attention at that point was mostly on the theatre. I made a promise to myself that I would make the FEU Auditorium the best professionally equipped theatre in the Philippines. To accomplish that, I presented a carefully prepared list of essentials for that purpose. I was lucky that the Board of Trustees approved my proposal. Once the approval was official, I copied the list of equipment that the Nichigeki Theatre had in Tokyo. Presentations at that theatre were called the

NUDE SHOW, which is no longer in existence. At that time, however, the beautiful nude women dancing there with scanty dazzling outfits covering their statuesque bodies looked well-dressed due to the magical combination of theatrical lights.

I had to work with the Sony Company who at that time did business only in Japan. On three consecutive summers I had to fly to Tokyo to buy from this company the most essential equipment for my purpose. I left the fancy ones for later years.

Mrs. Imelda Marcos happened to be buying the lighting equipment for the Cultural Center as well. We met in Tokyo and she asked me what I was buying and I showed her the list. She told the Sony people that she was buying exactly the same equipment. I told Mr. Yoshino of Sony to attend to Mrs. Marcos first as she was the First Lady of my country. So she received the shipment much earlier than FEU.

On the night of the dress rehearsal for the grand opening of the Cultural Center, Bert Avellana who was directing the show called me and opened the conversation with all the cuss words he could think of and remember. The equipment was so sophisticated that nobody knew how to run the blasted lighting system.

From the very first time I had planned to buy the equipment, I trained two of my brightest students on the modern control of stage lights which was done in those times by console. Today, of course, everything is done with computers. So I sent one of my trained students to help Bert.

In less than 2 years FEU got back all the money spent for the equipment of the stage because most of the foreign companies which put on shows chose our venue for their performances.

# Epilogue
*by Fred de la Rosa*

Mama joined us in 1977, several months after the family settled on 2077 8th Road, Arlington, Virginia. It was a reunion of sorts. Mama and I had known each other since my courtship of Baby. We shared a roof—her housin San Juan, Rizal—in the 1960s. She made me part of her family. Now she would be part of mine.

She came on a taxi one cold October afternoon. She had landed at the Baltimore Airport because of an error, took a shuttle to National, and there hailed a cab. She had no difficulty finding our place. I was not surprised. She had been an independent, enterprising woman all her life. She had lived and survived as a self-reliant, take-charge person.

She was traveling light because the airline lost her bags. She was not worried. An experienced traveler, she was confident the airline would find her suitcases and return them to her. She was happy to see us. And we—Baby, Dino, Freddie, Luigi and Lily, our loyal maid—were glad to welcome her.

After taking her rest, recovering from jet lag and adjusting to the place, she began to tell us about her plans. She wanted to work so she could earn a modest income. She wanted to look up her old chums, from the Catholic University, where she studied—Father Hartke, a former professor, was top on her list—to the State Department, where she had friends. Enrolling in a self-improvement course was part of her priorities. Getting back to the stage was a must. She wanted to be the cook for the family. And she wanted to learn how to drive.

We nodded to most of her plans, except the ones on work and on driving. She was in her sixties, after all, actually 69. She had a car in Manila but did not drive. Joey, her youngest son, took care of that. The stage, teaching, cooking and continuing studies, of course, were her passions. But we discouraged her from getting a job and taking over the wheels.

She slid easily into the rhythm of our daily life. She was very helpful with the boys' studies, breathed down Lily's neck at the kitchen and took care of general housekeeping. She tended the garden and looked after the lawn. The house began to have a sense of order. She declared war on the chaos that filled the rooms of Freddie and Luigi. She brought to the place the principles of sound organization.

Her suitcases came and her room, sparse at the beginning, began to fill up. Soon, her hobbies and interests began to attract a wealth of possessions: magazines from publishing houses and books from the *Book-of-the-Month Club*, letters from friends in the Philippines and the US. A sewing machine arrived, then a painting set. Her brother-in-law, National Artist Nick Joaquin, once referred to her as a dynamo and now, Sarah the dynamo was energizing the house and making her presence felt.

Her library began to grow. She was an avid reader. Initially she was reading Reader's Digest's condensed bestsellers—four abbreviated novels in each volume. She shared with me the classics: *Rebecca, Madame Bovary, Pride and Prejudice* and the Dickens collection. She loved the great plays, of course, from the Greek tragedies to the modern dramas.

Her love for books oozed from a flair for writing. In high school and college her teachers had enjoyed her juvenile compositions. She kept a diary on and off. She contributed to weekly magazines and weekend newspaper supplements in Manila. In Washington, she became a regular contributor to *Manila Mail*, the leading Filipino American weekly in the Virginia-DC-Maryland region. She wrote on a variety of subjects: art, culture, history, the mores, always with a sigh for nostalgia. Perhaps it was in the late 1990s or early in the 21$^{st}$ century that she decided to write her autobiography. No one knew about it. It was a surprise to us that she had written eighteen to twenty chapters before the curtain fell. But it did not surprise me that she would venture on such a project. She had a good memory, an eye for detail, and a knack for chronicling milestones in her life. An autobiography would crown her romance with the essay and her intermittent diary.

She loved to write. Nick writes:

> After the war she was with a theater group that put on plays like García Lorca's *House of Bernarda Alba*, and was criticized for not putting on native drama. So Sarah asked me to write them a play, a three-act play. I demurred I was no playwright and wouldn't know how to dramatize action or build up dialogue. "Just do what you can," said Sarah, "and I'll edit it." So I wrote *A Portrait of theArtist as Filipino*, with her in mind doing the starring role of Paula. Sarah went through the huge bundle of manuscript and shook her head. "But this is impossible! " she cried. I agreed with her and dumped my play on a shelf, where it gathered dust until discovered by Daisy Avellana. The rest, as they say, is history.

Mama's FM radio was glued to Washington's only classical-music radio station, WETA, if memory does not err. She had a weakness for waltzes and sonatas, her instruments of choice being the piano, the violin and the cello. She was a good marimba player and could coax a melody out of the piano. When I left Washington for Manila, she would tape her favorite music and mailed them to me. The cassettes were properly labeled, each piece identified, in her fine handwriting that mirrored affection and care.

If she wasn't cooking, she was busy knitting and sewing. She made socks, sweaters and mufflers. If she cared to and had the time, she would paint on some of her work. She had an aptitude for art. She gave away her knitting as gifts, which were highly appreciated.

Her cooking was divine, keyed, of course, to the Hispanic kitchen. She made great *paella*, *bacalao* and *lengua*. She baked goodies. When I was temporarily out of a job, I turned to her for cooking lessons. She was a messy cook and needed Dino to clean up her mess.

She built her possessions, properties and assets by earning a living.

Age did not stop her from looking for work, or welcoming work that came her way. We told her she did not have to work or worry about expenses. We were living modestly but comfortably. She insisted on using her talents and experience and making contributions to the household. We gave up. She endeared herself to a number of families who had babies and small children to look after. Some of her employers required stay-in arrangements, so we would miss her five days a week. Other couples brought their babies to the house, which was welcome. Initially she lied to her employers about her age, fearing they might not accept her at her age. Time, it turned out, was not a disqualifier. Soon word spread that there was this old Filipina lady who was a fine nanny, a good teacher, who was patient, warm and reliable. A grandmother who loved children.

Her reputation as a linguist had preceded her. *Kababayans* wishing to learn Spanish or brush up on the language started coming to the house for tutoring. She did translation for the Philippine Embassy and the State Department, putting into good service her fluency in Spanish, English and Filipino. She wrote in Spanish when corresponding with Nick Joaquin and other friends versed in the language of Cervantes.

Mama had a talent for fortune telling, telling people snippets from their past and future by reading their cards. Relatives, friends and associates in Manila sought her to divine their future and to ask for advice. In Washington, she built a legion of admirers from the Filipino American community, the diplomatic service and international organizations. They were so impressed by her ability to "read the cards" and they kept coming back. People would tell Baby and me how uncanny Mama was in peering into their fortune. She would end each session by telling a guest to ask a question that was answerable by yes or no. After laying out the cards, she could tell—with confidence—that the wish would or would not come true in varying degrees of difficulty.

I was "cautious" enough not to have Mama read my cards. I kidded her and Baby that there was much "classified information" in my life that needed protection. Baby skirted my reservations by asking Mama to read her cards. She thought this would help her know something about my future.

A number of World Bank and embassy executives sought Mama for private lessons in public speaking. In the 60s, she had prepped Eddie Ilarde—later TV host, congressman and senator—and other students for oratorical competitions. At FEU, she had taught voice development, diction and radio announcing. She knew the power of the spoken word, of projection and modulation. She imparted these gifts to business and civic executives who wanted to improve themselves and rise in their professions.

In the 1990s, she bought a computer to speed up her correspondence and writing schedule. She enrolled in a fiction-writing class that offered home-study lessons. The exercises challenged her imagination. She had not written fiction before. In her diary, she commented on the difficulties of intelligent plotting, dialogue, characterization and narration. She got mixed grades. I do not know if she ever wrote a short story or a novella.

Mama's health was unsteady, however. She had arthritis, heart palpitations, suffered shortness of breath. She had been a heavy smoker in early adulthood, but she never had—thank God—any problem with her lungs. At one time she weighed 149 pounds. On several occasions, we had to call *911* for help. The ambulance always arrived promptly in the evening, sneaking into the yard quietly, announcing its presence only with its blinking lights and the purr of the engine. Upon satisfying themselves that Mama needed hospital care, the orderlies would put her gently on a stretcher and drive into the night with her, Baby and I following behind in the family car.

She enjoyed TV quiz shows—Jeopardy! was her favorite—knew the latest football scores, attended socials and traveled whenever she could.

She played mahjong occasionally, loved to play tourist guide to visiting friends and relatives. She did crossword puzzles. And, yes...she enjoyed shopping.

Mama was also forgiving. She would not nurse grudges or anger for long. She was a soft touch for panhandlers and people asking for help. On being told that most beggars were opportunists or that people were taking advantage of her generous heart, she remarked, "*Hindi baling lokohin ako; basta nakatulong.* (They can play me for a dupe, I don't care as long as I can help)."

She lived by the biblical injunction on forgiveness. Her faith was strong and her obedience to her Maker was absolute. This showed not only in her churchgoing but also in her daily life. She had willed her life to God.

Mama fulfilled her dream to return to the stage. She acted in *Sisa* (1989) and *Anastasia* (1993) with Boots Anson Roa. She took part in a dramatic reading of Nick Joaquin's *Portrait of the Artist as Filipino*.

She directed *Why Women Wash the Dishes* (1993) and Joaquin's *May Day Eve* (1994), *Isang New Yorker sa Tondo* (1994) and *Sa Kahabaan ng Madilim na Gabi* (with Oscar Bonoan, Alice Santos and Egai Detera). In 1995 she directed three one-act plays: *Ang Mundo ay Isang Mansanas, Kamatayan ng Isang Duwag* and *Panhik-Ligaw* (with Jon Melegrito and Irma Montero).

In 1995 she directed, at 87, the classic three-act zarzuela *Ang Kiri (The Coquette)*, the first-ever zarzuela to be staged in the Washington region, performed at the Duke Ellington School of the Arts in Washington, DC. Written by Servando de los Reyes with music by Leon Ignacio, *Ang Kiri* offers great music and melodic songs within a simple love story. The Washington production starred Evelyn Mandac, the noted Filipino soprano, and Hubert Santayana.

In the Philippines and the US, she won numerous awards and appreciations. Among those who have honored her were the Far Eastern University (Lifetime Achievement Award, 1994); the Virginia-based Forex Group of Companies; Tanghalang Pilipino (1989); the Filipino American Community of Northern Virginia (1987); the Philippine Embassy (1993); the Filipino American Women's Network (1994); Asian American Chamber of Commerce (1996); Philippine Festival Centennial Committee (1998); and the Filipino American Senior Citizens Group (1998).

Warm accolades came from friends, peers, actors and students who had worked with her. Ray Pedroche, former broadcast professional and currently a teacher, confesses: "The reason, the main one, why I enrolled at the Far Eastern University (and not at UP where my father CV, the writer, graduated) was because of Sarah, truth to tell. And when I had to climb five flights of stairs at the Science Building to get to the broadcast studio where we held classes, I did not mind it at all because I sensed that I was going to like it there and I belonged there."

Pedroche recalls how Mama taught him and other drama students at the FEU when the school was famous for its plays and musicals, when the FEU Auditorium was the dominant landmark on the cultural scene. "Sarah's mere presence made things light up," Pedroche says. "It was showtime all the time she was around. She did not teach the way a teacher taught. She showed. She lived. She loved." And she showered every actor with her favorite expletive: *puñeta*.

"Sarah was my second mother," sighs Joan Orendain, the public relations pundit. Mama had directed her in a play with Noel Trinidad. Joan recalls spending nights at the Joaquin home for rehearsals or when she felt like it.

Death overtook her on January 30, 2002, in Falls Church, Virginia, three weeks after her 94th birthday. She had been at the hospital for some time, but the family was hopeful about her recovery. She was cremated, as she had wished. Her body dissolved into ashes, but not her work and her life.

In her lifetime, Sarah K. Joaquin had become a forceful presence on the stage—acting, directing, writing and teaching drama. She is part of the great theater tradition that began in the 1800s and continues to flourish today. She was a founding member of the Barangay Theater Guild, member of the Manila Theater Guild, Dramatic Philippines and drama director at FEU for many decades.

She inspired generations of students to finish their studies and succeed in their profession. She helped them discover the magic of language, Spanish or English, the wonders of the stage and the beauty of teaching. A great number of students became radio hosts, TV announcers, actors, singers and directors.

It must be said that she inspired a future writer and a national artist, Nick Joaquin, who acknowledged her tutorship, guidance, and who gave him the critical "break" that helped launch his literary life.

She was a big help to Baby and our children—Dino, Freddie and Luigi, and later to her grandchildren: Diego, Noah, Elijah, Mateo and Marco Joaquin and their mothers, Zinnia and Monica. She made our life full and complete in the 25 years she stayed with us.

Jestingly, I introduced her to friends as "my favorite mother-in-law." She replied by referring to me as "my favorite son-in-law." She was the mother I missed most of my life. My own mother died when I was eight.

One wintry afternoon, as we were about to cross a snow-covered corner of Annandale Road, I offered her an arm and said, "Ma, the ice is slippery. Take a strong grip lest you slip and fall."

She took my arm and we crossed the street. It was I who slipped and I landed on my behind. She helped me up, both of us laughing.

That incident summarized her role in our lives. She was a pillar of strength and support. She was there when we needed her. I believe she continues to pray for us.

Sarah Joaquin demonstrated that age cannot wither the spirit or make enthusiasm stale. Nick Joaquin paid her the highest accolade: "When I think of Sarah I see dynamos. Physically, intellectually, spiritually, she's a dynamo. And I speak from a knowledge of her dating back to my childhood. I'm happy to hear she is still effervescing. I doubt she'll ever burn out!"

Mama's ashes were flown to Manila in March 2002. She had wanted to be buried in her homeland. She got her wish. The editorial comments in the Manila press paid tribute to her devotion to teaching and the stage. The Far Eastern University, home for many years, held a commemorative Mass and invited friends, admirers, colleagues former students and people who have heard of Sarah K. Joaquin to take part in a final tribute. They responded in droves, at the FEU and at the burial, recalling her life and her work, acknowledging her influence on their vocation, joining hands for a final ovation for a great human being.